Symbolic Interactionism

Symbolic Interactionism
Perspective and Method

HERBERT BLUMER
University of California, Berkeley

Prentice-Hall, Inc. / Englewood Cliffs, New Jersey

13–879924–5

Library of Congress Catalog Card No.: 76–80731

Current printing (last digit):

10 9 8 7 6 5 4 3 2 1

Printed in the United States of America

PRENTICE-HALL INTERNATIONAL, INC., *London*
PRENTICE-HALL OF AUSTRALIA, PTY. LTD., *Sydney*
PRENTICE-HALL OF CANADA, LTD., *Toronto*
PRENTICE-HALL OF INDIA PRIVATE LTD., *New Delhi*
PRENTICE-HALL OF JAPAN, INC., *Tokyo*

To My Daughter, Katherine Hade

Preface

The present volume is being published in response to many requests from former students and from professional colleagues whom I have not been privileged to have as students. They have asked that I make available to them in a single book several of my articles now scattered in different publications, indicating that such an arrangement would be beneficial to them and to their students. In responding to their requests I have selected from my articles those which deal with aspects of symbolic interactionism or with methodological problems. These two areas of scholarly interest have been of major concern to me since my graduate days, when I wrote a doctoral dissertation on "Method in Social Psychology." The linking of these two concerns is not a marriage of convenience however but a genuine union. It is my conviction that an empirical science necessarily has to respect the nature of the empirical world that is its object of study. In my judgment symbolic interactionism shows that respect for the nature of human group life and conduct. But that respect necessitates, in turn, the development of a methodological perspective congruent with the nature of the empirical world under study.

Various of my articles, chiefly those brought together in this volume, touch in one way or another on the point of view of symbolic interactionism or on methodological matters related to that point of view. I wrote each of these articles, however, for a specific purpose. Thus, even when grouped together they do not give the unified picture I have sought to present to graduate students over four decades of instruction. In a partial effort to fill this need I have prepared a lengthy introductory essay for the present volume. This essay is the only previously unpublished body of writing in the volume. I recommend that the essay be read first in order to grasp the import of any of the subsequent articles.

I wish to thank those of my former students who spurred and prodded me to publish this volume. They are many, and it would be pretentious to list their names. I feel called on, however, to single out the two who have been most persistent over the years in making this request: Tamotsu Shibutani and Howard Becker. To their names I add that of my friend James Clark, formerly of Prentice-Hall, who above all has pressed me gently but unrelentingly to bring out this set of my writings. In the light of these solicitations I can honestly disclaim responsibility if the publication of the present volume becomes an unsuccessful venture.

HERBERT BLUMER

Berkeley, California

Contents

Symbolic Interactionism

1

The Methodological Position
of Symbolic Interactionism

The term "symbolic interactionism" has come into use as a label for a relatively distinctive approach to the study of human group life and human conduct.* The scholars who have used the approach or contributed to its intellectual foundation are many, and include such notable American figures as George Herbert Mead, John Dewey, W. I. Thomas, Robert E. Park, William James, Charles Horton Cooley, Florian Znaniecki, James Mark Baldwin, Robert Redfield, and Louis Wirth. Despite significant differences in the thought of such scholars, there is a great similarity in the general way in which they viewed and studied human group life. The concept of symbolic interactionism is built around this strand of general similarity. There has been no clear formulation of the position of symbolic interactionism, and above all, a reasoned statement of the methodological position of this approach is lacking. This essay is an effort to develop such a statement. I rely chiefly on the thought of George Herbert Mead who, above all others, laid the foundations of the symbolic interactionist approach, but I have been compelled to develop my own version, dealing explicitly with many crucial matters that were only implicit in the thought of Mead and others, and

* The term "symbolic interactionism" is a somewhat barbaric neologism that I coined in an offhand way in an article written in MAN AND SOCIETY (Emerson P. Schmidt, ed. New York: Prentice-Hall, 1937). The term somehow caught on and is now in general use.

1

covering critical topics with which they were not concerned. Thus, to a major extent I must bear full responsibility for the views and analyses presented here. This is especially true of my treatment of methodology; the discussion of this topic is solely my own. My scheme of treatment is first to outline the nature of symbolic interactionism, next to identify the guiding principles of methodology in the case of empirical science, and finally to deal specifically with the methodological position of symbolic interactionism.

THE NATURE OF SYMBOLIC INTERACTIONISM

Symbolic interactionism rests in the last analysis on three simple premises. The first premise is that human beings act toward things on the basis of the meanings that the things have for them. Such things include everything that the human being may note in his world—physical objects, such as trees or chairs; other human beings, such as a mother or a store clerk; categories of human beings, such as friends or enemies; institutions, as a school or a government; guiding ideals, such as individual independence or honesty; activities of others, such as their commands or requests; and such situations as an individual encounters in his daily life. The second premise is that the meaning of such things is derived from, or arises out of, the social interaction that one has with one's fellows. The third premise is that these meanings are handled in, and modified through, an interpretative process used by the person in dealing with the things he encounters. I wish to discuss briefly each of these three fundamental premises.

It would seem that few scholars would see anything wrong with the first premise—that human beings act toward things on the basis of the meanings which these things have for them. Yet, oddly enough, this simple view is ignored or played down in practically all of the thought and work in contemporary social science and psychological science. Meaning is either taken for granted and thus pushed aside as unimportant or it is regarded as a mere neutral link between the factors responsible for human behavior and this behavior as the product of such factors. We can see this clearly in the predominant posture of psychological and social science today. Common to both of these fields is the tendency to treat human behavior as the product of various factors that play upon human beings; concern is with the behavior and with the factors regarded as producing them. Thus, psychologists turn to such factors as stimuli, attitudes, conscious or unconscious motives, various kinds of psychological inputs, perception and cognition, and various features of personal organization to account for given forms or instances of human conduct. In a similar fashion sociologists rely on such factors as social position, status demands, social roles, cultural prescriptions, norms and values, social pressures, and group affiliation to provide such explanations. In both such typical psychological and sociological explanations the meanings of things for the human beings who are acting are either bypassed or swallowed up in the factors used to account for their behavior. If one declares that the given kinds of behavior are the result of the particular factors regarded as producing them, there is no need to concern oneself with the meaning of the things toward which human beings act; one merely identifies the initiating factors and the resulting behavior. Or one may, if pressed, seek to accommodate the element of meaning by lodging it in the initiating factors or by regarding it as a neutral link intervening between the initiating factors and the behavior they are alleged to produce. In the first of these latter cases the meaning disappears by being merged into the initiating or causative factors; in the second case meaning becomes a mere transmission link that can be ignored in favor of the initiating factors.

The position of symbolic interactionism, in contrast, is that the meanings that things have for human beings are central in their own right. To ignore the meaning of the things toward which people act is seen as falsifying the behavior under study. To bypass the meaning in favor of factors alleged to produce the behavior is seen as a grievous neglect of the role of meaning in the formation of behavior.

The simple premise that human beings act toward things on the basis of the meaning of such things is much too simple in itself to differentiate symbolic interactionism—there are several other approaches that share this premise. A major line of difference between them and symbolic interactionism is set by the second premise, which refers to the source of meaning. There are two well-known traditional ways of accounting for the origin of meaning. One of them is to regard meaning as being intrinsic to the thing that has it, as being a natural part of the objective makeup of the thing. Thus, a chair is clearly a chair in itself, a cow a cow, a cloud a cloud, a rebellion a rebellion, and so forth. Being inherent in the thing that has it, meaning needs merely to be disengaged by observing the objective thing that has the meaning. The meaning emanates, so to speak, from the thing and as such there is no process involved in its formation; all that is necessary is to recognize the meaning that is there in the thing. It should be immediately apparent that this view reflects the traditional position of "realism" in philosophy—a position that is widely held and deeply entrenched in the social and psychological sciences. The other major traditional view regards "meaning" as a psychical accretion brought to the thing by the person for whom the thing has meaning. This psychical accretion is treated as being an expression of constituent elements of the person's psyche, mind, or psychological organization. The constituent elements are such things as sensations, feelings, ideas, memories, motives, and attitudes. The meaning of a thing is but the expression of the given psychological elements that are brought into play in connection with the perception of the thing; thus one seeks to explain the meaning of a thing by isolating the particular psychological elements that produce the meaning. One sees this in the somewhat ancient and classical psychological practice of analyzing the meaning of an object by identifying the sensations that enter into perception of that object; or in the contemporary practice of tracing the meaning of a thing, such as let us say prostitution, to the attitude of the person who views it. This lodging of the meaning of things in psychological elements limits the processes of the formation of meaning to whatever processes are involved in arousing and bringing together the given psychological elements that produce the meaning. Such processes are psychological in nature, and include perception, cognition, repression, transfer of feelings, and association of ideas.

Symbolic interactionism views meaning as having a different source than those held by the two dominant views just considered. It does not regard meaning as emanating from the intrinsic makeup of the thing that has meaning, nor does it see meaning as arising through a coalescence of psychological elements in the person. Instead, it sees meaning as arising in the process of interaction between people. The meaning of a thing for a person grows out of the ways in which other persons act toward the person with regard to the thing. Their actions operate to define the thing for the person. Thus, symbolic interactionism sees meanings as social products, as creations that are formed in and through the defining activities of people as they interact. This point of view gives symbolic interactionism a very distinctive position, with profound implications that will be discussed later.

The third premise mentioned above further differentiates symbolic interactionism. While the meaning of things is formed in the context of social interaction and is derived by the person from that interaction, it is a mistake to think that the use of meaning by a person is but an application of the meaning so derived. This mistake seriously mars the work of many scholars who otherwise follow the symbolic interactionist approach. They fail to see that the use of meanings by a person in his action involves an interpretative process. In this respect they are similar to the adherents of the two dominant views spoken of above—to those who lodge meaning in the objective makeup of the thing that has it and those who regard it as an expression of psychological elements. All three are alike in viewing the use of meaning by the human being in his action as being no more than an arousing and application of already established meanings. As such, all three fail to see that the use of meanings by the actor occurs through *a process of interpretation.* This process has two distinct steps. First, the actor indicates to himself the things toward which he is acting; he has to point out to himself the things that have meaning. The making of such indications is an internalized social process in that the actor is interacting with himself. This interaction with himself is something other than an interplay of psychological elements; it is an instance of the person engaging in a process of communication with himself. Second, by virtue of this process of communicating with himself, interpretation becomes a matter of handling meanings. The actor selects, checks, suspends, regroups, and transforms the meanings in the light of the situation in which he is placed and the direction of his action. Accordingly, interpretation should not be regarded as a mere automatic application of established meanings but as a formative process in which meanings are used and revised as instruments for the guidance and formation of action. It is necessary to see that meanings play their part in action through a process of self-interaction.

It is not my purpose to discuss at this point the merits of the three views that lodge meaning respectively in the thing, in the psyche, and in social action, nor to elaborate on the contention that meanings are handled flexibly by the actor in the course of forming his action. Instead, I wish merely to note that by being based on these three premises, symbolic interaction is necessarily led to develop an analytical scheme of human society and human conduct that is quite distinctive. It is this scheme that I now propose to outline.

Symbolic interactionism is grounded on a number of basic ideas, or "root images," as I prefer to call them. These root images refer to and depict the nature of the following matters: human groups or societies, social interaction, objects, the human being as an actor, human action, and the interconnection of the lines of action. Taken together, these root images represent the way in which symbolic interactionism views human society and conduct. They constitute the framework of study and analysis. Let me describe briefly each of these root images.

NATURE OF HUMAN SOCIETY OR HUMAN GROUP LIFE. Human groups are seen as consisting of human beings who are engaging in action. The action consists of the multitudinous activities that the individuals perform in their life as they encounter one another and as they deal with the succession of situations confronting them. The individuals may act singly, they may act collectively, and they may act on behalf of, or as representatives of, some organization or group of others. The activities belong to the acting individuals and are carried on by them always with regard to the situations in which they have to act. The import of this simple and essentially redundant characterization is that fundamentally human groups or society *exists in action* and must be seen in terms of action. This picture of human society as action must be the starting point (and the point of return) for any scheme that purports to treat and analyze human society empirically. Conceptual schemes that depict society in some other fashion can only be derivations from the complex of ongoing activity that constitutes group life. This is true of the two dominant conceptions of society in contemporary sociology—that of culture and that of social structure. Culture as a conception, whether defined as custom, tradition, norm, value, rules, or such like, is clearly derived from what people do. Similarly, social structure in any of its aspects, as represented by such terms as social position, status, role, authority, and prestige, refers to relationships derived from how people act toward each other. The life of any human society consists necessarily of an ongoing process of fitting together the activities of its members. It is this complex of ongoing activity that establishes and portrays structure or organization. A cardinal principle of symbolic interactionism is that any empirically oriented scheme of human society, however derived, must respect the fact that in the first and last instances human society consists of people engaging in action. To be empirically valid the scheme must be consistent with the nature of the social action of human beings.

NATURE OF SOCIAL INTERACTION. Group life necessarily presupposes interaction between the group members; or, put otherwise, a society consists of individuals interacting with one another. The activities of the members occur predominantly in response to one another or in relation to one another. Even though this is recognized almost universally in definitions of human society, social interaction is usually taken for granted and treated as having little, if any, significance in its own right. This is evident in typical sociological and psychological schemes—they treat social interaction as merely a medium through which the determinants of behavior pass to produce the behavior. Thus, the typical sociological scheme ascribes behavior to such factors as status position, cultural prescriptions, norms, values, sanctions, role demands, and social system requirements; explanation in terms of such factors suffices without paying attention to the social interaction that their play necessarily presupposes. Similarly, in the typical psychological scheme such factors as motives, attitudes, hidden complexes, elements of psychological organization, and psychological processes are used to account for behavior without any need of considering social interaction. One jumps from such causative factors to the behavior they are supposed to produce. Social interaction becomes a mere forum through which sociological or psychological determinants move to bring about given forms of human behavior. I may add that this ignoring of social interaction is not corrected by speaking of an interaction of societal elements (as when a sociologist speaks of an interaction of social roles or an interaction between the components of a social system) or an interaction of psychological elements (as when a psychologist speaks of an interaction between the attitudes held by different people). Social interaction is an interaction between actors and not between factors imputed to them.

Symbolic interactionism does not merely give a ceremonious nod to social interaction. It recognizes social interaction to be of vital importance in its own right. This importance lies in the fact that social interaction is a process that *forms* human conduct instead of being merely a means or a setting for the expression or release of human conduct. Put simply, human beings in interacting with one another have to take account of what each other is doing or is about to do; they are forced to direct their own conduct or handle their situations in terms of what they take into account. Thus, the activities of others enter as positive factors in the formation of their own conduct; in the face of the actions of others one may abandon an intention or purpose, revise it, check or suspend it, intensify it, or replace it. The actions of others enter to set what one plans to do, may oppose or prevent such plans, may require a revision of such plans, and may demand a very different set of such plans. One has to *fit* one's own line of activity in some manner to the actions of others. The actions of others have to be taken into account and cannot be regarded as merely an arena for the expression of what one is disposed to do or sets out to do.

We are indebted to George Herbert Mead for the most penetrating analysis of social interaction—an analysis that squares with the realistic account just given. Mead identifies two forms or levels of social interaction in human society. He refers to them respectively as "the conversation of gestures" and "the use of significant symbols"; I shall term them respectively "non-symbolic interaction" and "symbolic interaction." Non-symbolic interaction takes place when one responds directly to the action of another without interpreting that action; symbolic interaction involves interpretation of the action. Non-symbolic interaction is most readily apparent in reflex responses, as in the case of a boxer who automatically raises his arm to parry a blow. However, if the boxer were reflectively to identify the forthcoming blow from his opponent as a feint designed to trap him, he would be engaging in symbolic interaction. In this case, he would endeavor to ascertain the meaning of the blow—that is, what the blow signifies as to his opponent's plan. In their association human beings engage plentifully in non-symbolic interaction as they respond immediately and unreflectively to each other's bodily movements, expressions, and tones of voice, but their characteristic mode of interaction is on the symbolic level, as they seek to understand the meaning of each other's action.

Mead's analysis of symbolic interaction is highly important. He sees it as a presentation of gestures and a response to the meaning of those gestures. A gesture is any part or aspect of an ongoing action that signifies the larger act of which it is a part—for example, the shaking of a fist as an indication of a possible attack, or the declaration of war by a nation as an indication of a posture and line of action of that nation. Such things as requests, orders, commands, cues, and declarations are gestures that convey to the person who recognizes them an idea of the intention and plan of forthcoming action of the individual who presents them. The person who responds organizes his response on the basis of what the gestures mean to him; the person who presents the gestures advances them as indications or signs of what he is planning to do as well as of what he wants the respondent to do or understand. Thus, the gesture has meaning for both the person who makes it and for the person to whom it is directed. When the gesture has the same meaning for both, the two parties understand each other. From this brief account it can be seen that the meaning of the gesture flows out along three lines (Mead's triadic nature of meaning): It signifies what the person to whom it is directed is to do; it signifies what the person who is making the gesture plans to do; and it signifies the joint action that is to arise by the articulation of the acts of both. Thus, for illustration, a robber's command to his victim to put up his hands is (a) an indication of what the victim is to do; (b) an indication of what the robber plans to do, that is, relieve the victim of his money; and (c) an indication of the joint act being formed, in this case a holdup. If there is confusion or misunderstanding along any one of these three lines of meaning, communication is ineffective, interaction is impeded, and the formation of joint action is blocked.

One additional feature should be added to round out Mead's analysis of symbolic interaction, namely, that the parties to such interaction must necessarily take each other's roles. To indicate to another what he is to do, one has to make the indication from the standpoint of that other; to order the victim to put up his hands the robber has to see this response in terms of the victim making it. Correspondingly, the victim has to see the command from the standpoint of the robber who gives the command; he has to grasp the intention and forthcoming action of the robber. Such mutual role-taking is the *sine qua non* of communication and effective symbolic interaction.

The central place and importance of symbolic interaction in human group life and conduct should be apparent. A human society or group consists of people in association. Such association exists necessarily in the form of people acting toward one another and thus engaging in social interaction. Such interaction in human society is characteristically and predominantly on the symbolic level; as individuals acting individually, collectively, or as agents of some organization encounter one another they are necessarily required to take account of the actions of one another as they form their own action. They do this by a dual process of indicating to others how to act and of interpreting the indications made by others. Human group life is a vast process of such defining to others what to do and of interpreting their definitions; through this process people come to fit their activities to one another and to form their own individual conduct. Both such joint activity and individual conduct are formed *in* and *through* this ongoing process; they are not mere expressions or products of what people bring to their interaction or of conditions that are antecedent to their interaction. The failure to accommodate to this vital point constitutes the fundamental deficiency of schemes that seek to account for human society in terms of social organization or psychological factors, or of any combination of the two. By virtue of symbolic interaction, human group life is necessarily a formative process and not a mere arena for the expression of pre-existing factors.

NATURE OF OBJECTS. The position of symbolic interactionism is that the "worlds" that exist for human beings and for their groups are composed of "objects" and that these objects are the product of symbolic interaction. An object is anything that can be indicated, anything that is pointed to or referred to—a cloud, a book, a legislature, a banker, a religious doctrine, a ghost, and so forth. For purposes of convenience one can classify objects in three categories: (a) physical objects, such as chairs, trees, or bicycles; (b) social objects, such as students, priests, a president, a mother, or a friend; and (c) abstract objects, such as moral principles, philosophical doctrines, or ideas such as justice, exploitation, or compassion. I repeat that an object is anything that can be indicated or referred to. The nature of an object—of any and every object—consists of the meaning that it has for the person for whom it is an object. This meaning sets the way in which he sees the object, the way in which he is prepared to act toward it, and the way in which he is ready to talk about it. An object may have a different meaning for different individuals: a tree will be a different object to a botanist, a lumberman, a poet, and a home gardener; the President of the United States can be a very different object to a devoted member of his political party than to a member of the opposition; the members of an ethnic group may be seen as a different kind of object by members of other groups. The meaning of objects for a person arises fundamentally out of the way they are defined to him by others with whom he interacts. Thus, we come to learn through the indications of others that a chair is a chair, that doctors are a certain kind of professional, that the United States Constitution is a given kind of legal document, and so forth. Out of a process of mutual indications common objects emerge—objects that have the same meaning for a given set of people and are seen in the same manner by them.

Several noteworthy consequences follow from the foregoing discussion of objects. First, it gives us a different picture of the environment or milieu of human beings. From their standpoint the environment consists *only* of the objects that the given human beings recognize and know. The nature of this environment is set by the meaning that the objects composing it have for those human beings. Individuals, also groups, occupying or living in the same spatial location may have, accordingly, very different environments; as we say, people may be living side by side yet be living in different worlds. Indeed, the term "world" is more suitable than the word "environment" to designate the setting, the surroundings, and the texture of things that confront them. It is the world of their objects with which people have to deal and toward which they develop their actions. It follows that in order to understand the action of people it is necessary to identify their world of objects—an important point that will be elaborated later.

Second, objects (in the sense of their meaning) must be seen as social creations—as being formed in and arising out of the process of definition and interpretation as this process takes place in the interaction of people. The meaning of anything and everything has to be formed, learned, and transmitted through a process of indication —a process that is necessarily a social process. Human group life on the level of symbolic interaction is a vast process in which people are forming, sustaining, and transforming the objects of their world as they come to give meaning to objects. Objects have no fixed status except as their meaning is sustained through indications and definitions that people make of the objects. Nothing is more apparent than that objects in all categories can undergo change in their meaning. A star in the sky is a very different object to a modern astrophysicist than it was to a sheepherder of biblical times; marriage was a different object to later Romans than to earlier Romans; the president of a nation who fails to act successfully through critical times may become a very different object to the citizens of his land. In short, from the standpoint of symbolic interactionism human group life is a process in which objects are being created, affirmed, transformed, and cast aside. The life and action of people necessarily change in line with the changes taking place in their world of objects.

THE HUMAN BEING AS AN ACTING ORGANISM. Symbolic interactionism recognizes that human beings must have a makeup that fits the nature of social interaction. The human being is seen as an organism that not only responds to others on the non-symbolic level but as one that makes indications to others and interprets their indications. He can do this, as Mead has shown so emphatically, only by virtue of possessing a "self." Nothing esoteric is meant by this expression. It means merely that a human being can be an object of his own action. Thus, he can recognize himself, for instance, as being a man, young in age, a student, in debt, trying to become a doctor, coming from an undistinguished family and so forth. In all such instances he is an object to himself; and he acts toward himself and guides himself in his actions toward others on the basis of the kind of object he is to himself. This notion of oneself as an object fits into the earlier discussion of objects. Like other objects, the self-object emerges from the process of social interaction in which other people are defining a person to himself. Mead has traced the way in which this occurs in his discussion of role-taking. He points out that in order to become an object to himself a person has to see himself from the outside. One can do this only by placing himself in the position of others and viewing himself or acting toward himself from that position. The roles the person takes range from that of discrete individuals (the "play stage"), through that of discrete organized groups (the "game stage") to that of the abstract community (the "generalized other"). In taking such roles the person is in a position to address or approach himself—as in the case of a young girl who in "playing mother" talks to herself as her mother would do, or in the case of a young priest who sees himself through the eyes of the priesthood. We form our objects of ourselves through such a process of role-taking. It follows that we see ourselves through the way in which others see or define us—or, more precisely, we see ourselves by taking one of the three types of roles of others that have been mentioned. That one forms an object of himself through the ways in which others define one to himself is recognized fairly well in the literature today, so despite its great significance I shall not comment on it further.

There is an even more important matter that stems from the fact that the human being has a self, namely that this enables him to interact with himself. This interaction is not in the form of interaction between two or more parts of a psychological system, as between needs, or between emotions, or between ideas, or between the id and the ego in the Freudian scheme. Instead, the interaction is social—a form of communication, with the person addressing himself as a person and responding thereto. We can clearly recognize such interaction in ourselves as each of us notes that he is angry with himself, or that he has to spur himself on in his tasks, or that he reminds himself to do this or that, or that he is talking to himself in working out some plan of action. As such instances suggest, self-interaction exists fundamentally as a process of making indications to oneself. This process is in play continuously during one's waking life, as one notes and considers one or another matter, or observes this or that happening. Indeed, for the human being to be conscious or aware of anything is equivalent to his indicating the thing to himself—he is identifying it as a given kind of object and considering its relevance or importance to his line of action. One's waking life consists of a series of such indications that the person is making to himself, indications that he uses to direct his action.

We have, then, a picture of the human being as an organism that

13

interacts with itself through a social process of making indications to itself. This is a radically different view of the human being from that which dominates contemporary social and psychological science. The dominant prevailing view sees the human being as a complex organism whose behavior is a response to factors playing on the organization of the organism. Schools of thought in the social and psychological sciences differ enormously in which of such factors they regard as significant, as is shown in such a diverse array as stimuli, organic drives, need-dispositions, conscious motives, unconscious motives, emotions, attitudes, ideas, cultural prescriptions, norms, values, status demands, social roles, reference group affiliations, and institutional pressures. Schools of thought differ also in how they view the organization of the human being, whether as a kind of biological organization, a kind of psychological organization, or a kind of imported societal organization incorporated from the social structure of one's group. Nevertheless, these schools of thought are alike in seeing the human being as a responding organism, with its behavior being a product of the factors playing on its organization or an expression of the interplay of parts of its organization. Under this widely shared view the human being is "social" only in the sense of either being a member of social species, or of responding to others (social stimuli), or of having incorporated within it the organization of his group.

The view of the human being held in symbolic interactionism is fundamentally different. The human being is seen as "social" in a much more profound sense—in the sense of an organism that engages in social interaction with itself by making indications to itself and responding to such indications. By virtue of engaging in self-interaction the human being stands in a markedly different relation to his environment than is presupposed by the widespread conventional view described above. Instead of being merely an organism that responds to the play of factors on or through it, the human being is seen as an organism that has to deal with what it notes. It meets what it so notes by engaging in a process of self-indication in which it makes an object of what it notes, gives it a meaning, and uses the meaning as the basis for directing its action. Its behavior with regard to what it notes is not a response called forth by the presentation of what it notes but instead is an action that arises out of the interpretation made through the process of self-indication.

14

In this sense, the human being who is engaging in self-interaction is not a mere responding organism but an acting organism—an organism that has to mold a line of action on the basis of what it takes into account instead of merely releasing a response to the play of some factor on its organization.

NATURE OF HUMAN ACTION. The capacity of the human being to make indications to himself gives a distinctive character to human action. It means that the human individual confronts a world that he must interpret in order to act instead of an environment to which he responds because of his organization. He has to cope with the situations in which he is called on to act, ascertaining the meaning of the actions of others and mapping out his own line of action in the light of such interpretation. He has to construct and guide his action instead of merely releasing it in response to factors playing on him or operating through him. He may do a miserable job in constructing his action, but he has to construct it.

This view of the human being directing his action by making indications to himself stands sharply in contrast to the view of human action that dominates current psychological and social science. This dominant view, as already implied, ascribes human action to an initiating factor or a combination of such factors. Action is traced back to such matters as motives, attitudes, need-dispositions, unconscious complexes, stimuli configurations, status demands, role requirements, and situational demands. To link the action to one or more of such initiating agents is regarded as fulfilling the scientific task. Yet, such an approach ignores and makes no place for the process of self-interaction through which the individual handles his world and constructs his action. The door is closed to the vital process of interpretation in which the individual notes and assesses what is presented to him and through which he maps out lines of overt behavior prior to their execution.

Fundamentally, action on the part of a human being consists of taking account of various things that he notes and forging a line of conduct on the basis of how he interprets them. The things taken into account cover such matters as his wishes and wants, his objectives, the available means for their achievement, the actions and anticipated actions of others, his image of himself, and the likely result of a given line of action. His conduct is formed and guided through such a process of indication and interpretation. In this process, given lines of action may be started or stopped, they may be abandoned or postponed, they may be confined to mere planning or to an inner life of reverie, or if initiated, they may be transformed. My purpose is not to analyze this process but to call attention to its presence and operation in the formation of human action. We must recognize that the activity of human beings consists of meeting a flow of situations in which they have to act and that their action is built on the basis of what they note, how they assess and interpret what they note, and what kind of projected lines of action they map out. This process is not caught by ascribing action to some kind of factor (for example, motives, need-dispositions, role requirements, social expectations, or social rules) that is thought to initiate the action and propel it to its conclusion; such a factor, or some expression of it, is a matter the human actor takes into account in mapping his line of action. The initiating factor does not embrace or explain how it and other matters are taken into account in the situation that calls for action. One has to get inside of the defining process of the actor in order to understand his action.

This view of human action applies equally well to joint or collective action in which numbers of individuals are implicated. Joint or collective action constitutes the domain of sociological concern, as exemplified in the behavior of groups, institutions, organizations, and social classes. Such instances of societal behavior, whatever they may be, consist of individuals fitting their lines of action to one another. It is both proper and possible to view and study such behavior in its joint or collective character instead of in its individual components. Such joint behavior does not lose its character of being constructed through an interpretative process in meeting the situations in which the collectivity is called on to act. Whether the collectivity be an army engaged in a campaign, a corporation seeking to expand its operations, or a nation trying to correct an unfavorable balance of trade, it needs to construct its action through an interpretation of what is happening in its area of operation. The interpretative process takes place by participants making indications to one another, not merely each to himself. Joint or collective action is an outcome of such a process of interpretative interaction.

INTERLINKAGE OF ACTION. As stated earlier, human group life consists of, and exists in, the fitting of lines of action to each other by the members of the group. Such articulation of lines of action gives rise to and constitutes "joint action"—a societal organization of conduct of different acts of diverse participants. A joint action, while made up of diverse component acts that enter into its formation, is different from any one of them and from their mere aggregation. The joint action has a distinctive character in its own right, a character that lies in the articulation or linkage as apart from what may be articulated or linked. Thus, the joint action may be identified as such and may be spoken of and handled without having to break it down into the separate acts that comprise it. This is what we do when we speak of such things as marriage, a trading transaction, war, a parliamentary discussion, or a church service. Similarly, we can speak of the collectivity that engages in joint action without having to identify the individual members of that collectivity, as we do in speaking of a family, a business corporation, a church, a university, or a nation. It is evident that the domain of the social scientist is constituted precisely by the study of joint action and of the collectivities that engage in joint action.

In dealing with collectivities and with joint action one can easily be trapped in an erroneous position by failing to recognize that the joint action of the collectivity is an interlinkage of the separate acts of the participants. This failure leads one to overlook the fact that a joint action always has to undergo a process of formation; even though it may be a well-established and repetitive form of social action, each instance of it has to be formed anew. Further, this career of formation through which it comes into being necessarily takes place through the dual process of designation and interpretation that was discussed above. The participants still have to guide their respective acts by forming and using meanings.

With these remarks as a background I wish to make three observations on the implications of the interlinkage that constitutes joint action. I wish to consider first those instances of joint action that are repetitive and stable. The preponderant portion of social action in a human society, particularly in a settled society, exists in the form of recurrent patterns of joint action. In most situations in which people act toward one another they have in advance a firm understanding of how to act and of how other people will act. They share common and pre-established meanings of what is expected in the action of the participants, and accordingly each participant is able to guide his own behavior by such meanings. Instances of repetitive and pre-established forms of joint action are so frequent and common that it is easy to understand why scholars have viewed them as the essence or natural form of human group life. Such a view is especially apparent in the concepts of "culture" and "social order" that are so dominant in social science literature. Most sociological schemes rest on the belief that a human society exists in the form of an established order of living, with that order resolvable into adherence to sets of rules, norms, values, and sanctions that specify to people how they are to act in their different situations.

Several comments are in order with regard to this neat scheme. First, it is just not true that the full expanse of life in a human society, in any human society, is but an expression of pre-established forms of joint action. New situations are constantly arising within the scope of group life that are problematic and for which existing rules are inadequate. I have never heard of any society that was free of problems nor any society in which members did not have to engage in discussion to work out ways of action. Such areas of unprescribed conduct are just as natural, indigenous, and recurrent in human group life as are those areas covered by pre-established and faithfully followed prescriptions of joint action. Second, we have to recognize that even in the case of pre-established and repetitive joint action each instance of such joint action has to be formed anew. The participants still have to build up their lines of action and fit them to one another through the dual process of designation and interpretation. They do this in the case of repetitive joint action, of course, by using the same recurrent and constant meanings. If we recognize this, we are forced to realize that the play and fate of meanings are what is important, not the joint action in its established form. Repetitive and stable joint action is just as much a result of an interpretative process as is a new form of joint action that is being developed for the first time. This is not an idle or pedantic point; the meanings that underlie established and recurrent joint action are themselves subject to pressure as well as to reinforcement, to incipient dissatisfaction as well as to indifference; they may be challenged as well as affirmed, allowed to slip along without concern as well as subjected to infusions of new vigor. Behind the facade of the objectively perceived joint action the set of meanings that sustains that joint action has a life that the social scientists can ill afford to ignore. A gratuitous acceptance of the concepts of norms, values, social rules, and the like should not blind the social scientist to the fact that any one of them is subtended by a process of social interaction —a process that is necessary not only for their change but equally well for their retention in a fixed form. It is the social process in group life that creates and upholds the rules, not the rules that create and uphold group life.

The second observation on the interlinkage that constitutes joint action refers to the extended connection of actions that make up so much of human group life. We are familiar with these large complex networks of action involving an interlinkage and interdependency of diverse actions of diverse people—as in the division of labor extending from the growing of grain by the farmer to an eventual sale of bread in a store, or in the elaborate chain extending from the arrest of a suspect to his eventual release from a penitentiary. These networks with their regularized participation of diverse people by diverse action at diverse points yields a picture of institutions that have been appropriately a major concern of sociologists. They also give substance to the idea that human group life has the character of a system. In seeing such a large complex of diversified activities, all hanging together in a regularized operation, and in seeing the complementary organization of participants in well-knit interdependent relationships, it is easy to understand why so many scholars view such networks or institutions as self-operating entities, following their own dynamics and not requiring that attention be given to the participants within the network. Most of the sociological analyses of institutions and social organization adhere to this view. Such adherence, in my judgment, is a serious mistake. One should recognize what is true, namely, that the diverse array of participants occupying different points in the network engage in their actions at those points on the basis of using given sets of meanings. A network or an institution does not function automatically because of some inner dynamics or system requirements; it functions because people at different points do something, and what they do is a result of how they define the situation in which they are called on to act. A limited appreciation of this point is reflected today in some of the work on decision-making, but on the whole the point is grossly ignored. It is necessary to recognize that the sets of meanings that lead participants to act as they do at their stationed points in the network have their own setting in a localized process of social interaction—and that these meanings are formed, sustained, weakened, strengthened, or transformed, as the case may be, through a socially defining process. Both the functioning and the fate of institutions are set by this process of interpretation as it takes place among the diverse sets of participants.

A third important observation needs to be made, namely, that any instance of joint action, whether newly formed or long established, has necessarily arisen out of a background of previous actions of the participants. A new kind of joint action never comes into existence apart from such a background. The participants involved in the formation of the new joint action always bring to that formation the world of objects, the sets of meanings, and the schemes of interpretation that they already possess. Thus, the new form of joint action always emerges out of and is connected with a context of previous joint action. It cannot be understood apart from that context; one has to bring into one's consideration this linkage with preceding forms of joint action. One is on treacherous and empirically invalid grounds if he thinks that any given form of joint action can be sliced off from its historical linkage, as if its makeup and character arose out of the air through spontaneous generation instead of growing out of what went before. In the face of radically different and stressful situations people may be led to develop new forms of joint action that are markedly different from those in which they have previously engaged, yet even in such cases there is always some connection and continuity with what went on before. One cannot understand the new form without incorporating knowledge of this continuity into one's analysis of the new form. Joint action not only represents a horizontal linkage, so to speak, of the activities of the participants, but also a vertical linkage with previous joint action.

SUMMARY REMARKS. The general perspective of symbolic interactionism should be clear from our brief sketch of its root images. This approach sees a human society as people engaged in living. Such living is a process of ongoing activity in which participants are developing lines of action in the multitudinous situations they encounter. They are caught up in a vast process of interaction in which they have to fit their developing actions to one another. This process of interaction consists in making indications to others of what to do and in interpreting the indications as made by others. They live in worlds of objects and are guided in their orientation and action by the meaning of these objects. Their objects, including objects of themselves, are formed, sustained, weakened, and transformed in their interaction with one another. This general process should be seen, of course, in the differentiated character which it necessarily has by virtue of the fact that people cluster in different groups, belong to different associations, and occupy different positions. They accordingly approach each other differently, live in different worlds, and guide themselves by different sets of meanings. Nevertheless, whether one is dealing with a family, a boy's gang, an industrial corporation, or a political party, one must see the activities of the collectivity as being formed through a process of designation and interpretation.

METHODOLOGICAL PRINCIPLES OF EMPIRICAL SCIENCE

I am dealing with symbolic interactionism not as a philosophical doctrine* but as a perspective in empirical social science—as an approach designed to yield verifiable knowledge of human group life and human conduct. Accordingly, its methodological principles have to meet the fundamental requirements of empirical science. What are these requirements? Current thought and discussion of methodology in the social and psychological sciences are marked by much misunderstanding and confusion on these matters. I find it advisable to sketch several basic principles.

I shall begin with the redundant assertion that an empirical science presupposes the existence of an empirical world. Such an empirical world exists as something available for observation, study, and analysis. It *stands over against* the scientific observer, with a character that has to be dug out and established through observation,

---

* Symbolic interactionism provides the premises for a profound philosophy with a strong humanistic cast. In elevating the "self" to a position of paramount importance and in recognizing that its formation and realization occur through taking the roles of others with whom one is implicated in the joint activities of group life, symbolic interactionism provides the essentials for a provocative philosophical scheme that is peculiarly attuned to social experience. The outlines of this philosophy are sketched especially in the writings of George Herbert Mead and John Dewey.

study, and analysis. This empirical world must forever be the central point of concern. It is the point of departure and the point of return in the case of empirical science. It is the testing ground for any assertions made about the empirical world. "Reality" for empirical science exists only in the empirical world, can be sought only there, and can be verified only there.

In order that this bald yet indispensable declaration not be misunderstood let me insert a few words about the traditional positions of idealism and realism, since these philosophical positions profoundly influence scientific inquiry in current social and psychological science.

The traditional position of idealism is that the "world of reality" exists only in human experience and that it appears only in the form in which human beings "see" that world. I think that this position is incontestable. It is impossible to cite a single instance of a characterization of the "world of reality" that is not cast in the form of human imagery. Nothing is known to human beings except in the form of something that they may indicate or refer to. To indicate anything, human beings must see it from their perspective; they must depict it as it appears to them. In this sense no fault can be found with the contention that the empirical world necessarily exists always in the form of human pictures and conceptions of it. However, this does not shift "reality," as so many conclude, from the empirical world to the realm of imagery and conception. One errs if he thinks that since the empirical world can exist for human beings only in terms of images or conceptions of it, therefore reality must be sought in images or conceptions independent of an empirical world. Such a solipsistic position is untenable and would make empirical science impossible. The position is untenable because of the fact that the empirical world can "talk back" to our pictures of it or assertions about it—talk back in the sense of challenging and resisting, or not bending to, our images or conceptions of it. This resistance gives the empirical world an obdurate character that is the mark of reality. The fact that one can accommodate or resolve the resistance only by forming a new image or conception does not free the empirical world of its obdurate character. It is this obdurate character of the empirical world—its ability to resist and talk back—that both calls for and justifies empirical science. Fundamentally, empirical science is an enterprise that seeks to develop images and conceptions that can successfully handle and accommodate the resistance offered by the empirical world under study.

The recognition that the empirical world has an obdurate character with which one has to come to terms gives full justification to the realist's insistence that the empirical world has a "real" character. However, it is necessary to avoid two conceptions that have plagued traditional realism and that have seriously impaired its fruitfulness. One of these conceptions is that the obdurate character, or reality, of the empirical world is fixed or immutable in some ultimate form whose unearthing is the objective of empirical science. To the contrary, the history of empirical science shows that the reality of the empirical world appears in the "here and now" and is continuously recast with the achievement of new discoveries. The danger of the belief that the reality of the empirical world exists in a perpetually fixed form comes in the natural disposition to take existing knowledge of that reality as constituting the perpetual fixed form. Such a disposition, as history shows, can be a formidable blockade to new inquiry and new discovery. The second sterilizing conception is that the reality of the empirical world has to be seen and cast in terms of the findings of advanced physical science—a conception that has been particularly pernicious in its effect on social and psychological science. There is no warrant for this conception. The obdurate character of the empirical world is what it is found to be through careful and honest study. To force all of the empirical world to fit a scheme that has been devised for a given segment of that world is philosophical doctrinizing and does not represent the approach of genuine empirical science.

The proper picture of empirical science, in my judgment, is that of a collective quest for answers to questions directed to the resistant character of the given empirical world under study. One has to respect the obdurate character of *that* empirical world—this is indeed the cardinal principle of empirical science. Empirical science pursues its quest by devising images of the empirical world under study and by testing these images through exacting scrutiny of the empirical world. This simple observation permits us to put the topic of methodology in proper focus. Methodology refers to, or covers, the principles that underlie and guide the full process of studying the obdurate character of the given empirical world. There are three highly important points implied by this conception of methodology:

(1) methodology embraces the entire scientific quest and not merely some selected portion or aspect of that quest; (2) each part of the scientific quest as well as the complete scientific act, itself, has to fit the obdurate character of the empirical world under study; therefore, methods of study are subservient to that world and should be subject to test by it; and (3) the empirical world under study and not some model of scientific inquiry provides the ultimate and decisive answer to the test. I wish to elaborate each of these three points.

(1) To my mind a recognition that methodology applies to and covers all parts of the scientific act should be self-evident. The point needs to be asserted only because of an astonishing disposition in current social science to identify methodology with some limited portion of the act of scientific inquiry, and further, to give that portion a gratuitous parochial cast. Today "methodology" in the social sciences is regarded with depressing frequency as synonymous with the study of advanced quantitative procedures, and a "methodologist" is one who is expertly versed in the knowledge and use of such procedures. He is generally viewed as someone who casts study in terms of quantifiable variables, who seeks to establish relations between such variables by the use of sophisticated statistical and mathematical techniques, and who guides such study by elegant logical models conforming to special canons of "research design." Such conceptions are a travesty on methodology as the logical study of the principles underlying the conduct of scientific inquiry. The method of empirical science obviously embraces the full scope of the scientific act, including the starting premises as well as the full round of procedural steps contained in that act. All of these components are essential to scientific study and all of them need to be analyzed and respected in developing the principles of methodology. To understand this matter, let me identify the more important parts of scientific inquiry, parts that are indispensable to inquiry in empirical science.

(a) *The Possession and Use of a Prior Picture or Scheme of the Empirical World under Study.* As previously mentioned, this is an unavoidable prerequisite for any study of the empirical world. One can see the empirical world only through some scheme or image of it. The *entire act* of scientific study is oriented and shaped by the underlying picture of the empirical world that is

24

used. This picture sets the selection and formulation of problems, the determination of what are data, the means to be used in getting data, the kinds of relations sought between data, and the forms in which propositions are cast. In view of this fundamental and pervasive effect wielded on the entire act of scientific inquiry by the initiating picture of the empirical world, it is ridiculous to ignore this picture. The underlying picture of the empirical world is always capable of identification in the form of a set of premises. These premises are constituted by the nature given either explicitly or implicitly to the key objects that comprise the picture. The unavoidable task of genuine methodological treatment is to identify and assess these premises.

(b) *The Asking of Questions of the Empirical World and the Conversion of the Questions into Problems.* This constitutes the beginning of the act of inquiry. It is obvious that the kind of questions asked and the kind of problems posed set and guide the subsequent lines of inquiry. Accordingly, it is highly important for the methodologist to examine carefully and appraise critically how problems are selected and formulated. Superficiality, humdrum conventionality, and slavish adherence to doctrine in the selection and setting of problems constitute a well-known bane in empirical science.

(c) *Determination of the Data to be Sought and the Means to be Employed in Getting the Data.* Obviously, the data are set by the problem—which indicates the importance of being sure of the satisfactory character of the problem. Even though set by the problem, the data need to be constantly examined to see if they require a revision or rejection of the problem. Beyond this, it is important to recognize that the means used to get the data depend on the nature of the data to be sought. A reverse relation of allowing the method used in securing data to determine the nature of the data vitiates genuine empirical inquiry. These few observations suggest the clear need for careful and critical consideration of how data are to be determined and collected.

(d) *Determination of Relations Between the Data.* Since the establishment of connections between the data yield the findings of the study, it is highly important to be aware of how such connections are reached. This is true whether one arrives at the connections through judicious reflection on what one conceives might be significant relations or whether one relies on a mechanical procedure such as factorial analysis or a scheme of computer correlation.

(e) *Interpretation of the Findings.* This terminal step carries the scientist beyond the confines of the problem he has studied, since in making interpretations he has to relate his findings to an outside body of theory or to a set of conceptions that transcend the study he has made. This important terminal step particularly merits methodological scrutiny in the case of social and psychological science. It is at this point, speaking metaphorically, that new cards may be slipped into the deck, conferring on the interpretation an unwarranted "scientific" status merely because the preceding steps of the study have been well done. The outside body of theory or set of conceptions used to frame the interpretation may be untested and may be false.

(f) *The Use of Concepts.* Throughout the act of scientific inquiry concepts play a central role. They are significant elements in the prior scheme that the scholar has of the empirical world; they are likely to be the terms in which his problem is cast; they are usually the categories for which data are sought and in which the data are grouped; they usually become the chief means for establishing relations between data; and they are usually the anchor points in interpretation of the findings. Because of such a decisive role in scientific inquiry, concepts need especially to be subject to methodological scrutiny.

Any treatment of methodology worthy of its name has to cover the above matters since they are clearly the essential parts of the act of empirical inquiry in science. They must be covered not in the sense of advancing a given scheme of the empirical world, outlining a set of problems in it, deciding on the data and how they are to be secured, prefiguring the lines of connection to be sought, sketching the framework to be employed in making interpretations, and identifying the concepts to be used. Instead, they must be covered in the sense of developing the principles to be observed in doing these things in such a way as to respect and come to grips with the obdurate character of the empirical world under study.

It is in this sense that much of present-day methodology in the social and psychological sciences is inadequate and misguided. The overwhelming bulk of what passes today as methodology is made up of such preoccupations as the following: the devising and use of sophisticated research techniques, usually of an advanced statistical character; the construction of logical and mathematical models, all too frequently guided by a criterion of elegance; the elaboration of formal schemes on how to construct concepts and theories; valiant

26

application of imported schemes, such as input-output analysis, systems analysis, and stochastic analysis; studious conformity to the canons of research design; and the promotion of a particular procedure, such as survey research, as *the* method of scientific study. I marvel at the supreme confidence with which these preoccupations are advanced as the stuff of methodology. Many of these preoccupations, such as those stressing the need for statistical and quantitative techniques, are grossly inadequate on the simple ground that they deal with only a limited aspect of the full act of scientific inquiry, ignoring such matters as premises, problems, concepts, and so on. More serious is their almost universal failure to face the task of outlining the principles of how schemes, problems, data, connections, concepts, and interpretations are to be constructed *in the light of the nature of the empirical world under study.* The cited preoccupations represent an effort to develop a methodology independent of the obdurate character of the empirical world to which the methodology is to apply. This is not how methodology is developed in the case of empirical science. The principles that comprise the methodology of an empirical science have to cover the act of scientific inquiry, not in some detached logical form of its own, but in the form that such scientific inquiry must take in grappling with a given kind of empirical world. It is in this important sense that methodology in the social and psychological sciences cannot ignore such matters as how the empirical world is to be viewed, how problems are to be posed, how data are to be selected, how their relations are to be established, how such relations are to be interpreted, and how concepts are to be used.

(2) Recognizing that methodology embraces all of the important parts of the act of scientific inquiry, I wish now to state and stress a point of even greater importance for methodology. Every part of the act of scientific inquiry—and hence the full act itself—is subject to the test of the empirical world and has to be validated through such a test. Reality exists in the empirical world and not in the methods used to study that world; it is to be discovered in the examination of that world and not in the analysis or elaboration of the methods used to study that world. Methods are mere instruments designed to identify and analyze the obdurate character of the empirical world, and as such their value exists only in their suitability in enabling this task to be done. In this fundamental sense the procedures employed

in each part of the act of scientific inquiry should and must be assessed in terms of whether they respect the nature of the empirical world under study—whether what they signify or imply to be the nature of the empirical world is actually the case. Thus the underlying scheme of the empirical world used in the act of scientific inquiry needs to be critically examined to see whether it is true; the problems set for study need to be critically studied to see whether they are genuine problems *in the empirical world;* the data chosen need to be inspected to see if in fact they have in the empirical world the character given to them in the study; similarly, the empirical world has to be examined, independently of the study, to see if the relations staked out between the data are found in their asserted form; the interpretations of the findings, particularly since they arise from sources outside the study, need to be given empirical testing; and the concepts used throughout the course of the study are in special need of scrutiny to see if they match in the empirical world what they purport to refer to. Nothing less than this is called for in methodological treatment.

Yet it is evident that such scrutiny and assessment of scientific inquiry are rare in what is advanced today as methodology in the social and psychological sciences. Premises, problems, data, relations, interpretations, and concepts are almost always accepted as given and so spared direct examination in terms of the empirical world. Instead, current methodology stresses other ways of trying to establish the empirical validity of the schemes, problems, data, relations, concepts, and interpretations. These other ways that are advocated and widely used are the following: (a) adhering to a scientific protocol, (b) engaging in replication of research studies, (c) relying on the testing of hypotheses, and (d) employing so-called operational procedures. I wish to discuss each of these alternative schemes.

There is a widespread and deeply entrenched belief in the social and psychological sciences that faithful adherence to what is commonly accepted as the proper protocol of research procedure automatically yields results that are valid for the empirical world. The protocol of "proper" research procedure is well standardized in the social and psychological sciences; it is well represented by what we speak of today as the principles of research design. Such a protocol is presented to students as the model for research; it is used regularly by scholars and editors in assessing research studies; and it is used rather rigorously by fund-granting bodies in evaluating research proposals. All of this bespeaks a belief that faithful adherence to the protocol of research procedure is a guarantee that one is respecting the nature of the empirical world. It is, of course, no such guarantee at all. Inside of the "scientific protocol" one can operate unwittingly with false premises, erroneous problems, distorted data, spurious relations, inaccurate concepts, and unverified interpretations. There is no built-in mechanism in the protocol to test whether the premises, problems, data, relations, concepts, and interpretations are sustained by the nature of the empirical world.

This observation applies also to the reliance on the replication of studies using an established research protocol. Such replication does not satisfy the need of empirical validation of premises, problems, concepts, and the other anchor props of scientific study. Whether or not a replicated study following a given protocol yields the same results as an earlier study stands apart from the question of the valid empirical status of the premises, problems, data, relations, concepts, and interpretations that are used.

Undoubtedly, the chief means used in present-day social and psychological science to establish the empirical validity of one's approach is the testing of hypotheses. The reasoning here is simple. One starts with the construction of a scheme, theory, or model of the empirical world or area under study. The scheme, theory, or model represents the way in which one believes the empirical world to be structured and to operate. One then deduces from this scheme an assertion as to what one would expect to happen under such and such a set of empirical circumstances. This assertion is the hypothesis. One then arranges a study of a given empirical area that represents these circumstances. If the findings from such a study verify the hypothesis one assumes that the scheme, the model, or the theory from which the hypothesis has been drawn is empirically valid. Logically, this view rests on an "as if" notion; that is, one approaches the empirical world *as if* it had such and such a makeup, deduces narrow specific consequences as to what one would find if the empirical world had the makeup attributed to it, and then sees if in fact such consequences are to be found in the empirical world.

There is a measure of truth in this view—but only (a) if the hypothesis genuinely *epitomizes* the model or the theory from which it is deduced; and (b) if the testing of the hypothesis is followed by scrupulous search for negative empirical cases. All too frequently these conditions are not met in the social and psychological sciences. The hypothesis rarely embodies or reflects the theory or model so crucially that the theory or model rides or falls with the fate of the hypothesis being tested. Further, the testing of the hypothesis is distinctly inadequate if it is limited to the particular empirical situation that is circumscribed by the hypothesis; it is necessary to see whether it holds up in a series of other relevant empirical situations, varied as much as possible in their settings. Unless these two specified conditions are met, one is merely testing the hypothesis and not the model or theoretical scheme from which it is deduced. As we shall see later, and understand for very good reasons, theoretical schemes in the social and psychological sciences have been notorious for the ease with which hypotheses deduced from them are verified or, as occasionally happens, such schemes show a remarkable ability to maintain intact a virile status even though some deduced hypotheses are found not to be sustained. We can see this *ad nauseum* in such theoretical schemes as the doctrine of instincts, Watsonian behaviorism, Gestalt psychology, the stimulus-response conception, psychoanalysis, the input-output model, the organic conception of human society, cultural determinism, and structural functionalism. The advocates and adherents of such theoretical schemes never have difficulty in verifying the hypotheses they draw from their schemes. Nor do I find that those schemes that are now passé disappeared because of discoveries that hypotheses deduced from them did not stand up. The causes of their disappearance must be sought in other sources. These observations should lead one to be very wary of the widespread reliance in social and psychological sciences on the testing of the hypothesis as the means of determining the empirical validity of theoretical schemes and models. There are grave grounds, merely on the basis of the record, for doubting the efficacy of this procedure, in social and psychological sciences, in establishing the empirical validity of premises, problems, data, relations, concepts, and interpretations.

The final type of procedure—the so-called operational procedure —is even less suitable for establishing the empirical validity of key anchor points in the act of scientific inquiry. "Operational procedure" rests on the idea that a theoretical assertion or a concept can be given both empirical reference and validation by developing a specific, regularized procedure for approaching the empirical world. The given procedure or operation may be the use of a test, a scale, a measuring instrument, or a standardized mode of inquiry. The procedure "operationalizes" the theoretical proposition or concept. If the given operation meets tests of reliability the operation is taken as a sound instrument for disengaging specific empirical data. In turn, these data are thought to be valid empirical referents of the concept or proposition that is operationalized. The use of intelligence tests is a classic example of operational procedure—the tests are reliable and standardized instruments; they yield clean-cut empirical data capable of replication; and the data (the intelligence quotients) can be justly regarded as constituting sound and valid empirical references of the concept of intelligence. Actually, a little careful reflection shows that operational procedure is not at all an empirical validation of what is being operationalized. The concept or proposition that is being operationalized, such as the concept of intelligence, refers to something that is regarded as present in the empirical world in diverse forms and diverse settings. Thus, as an example, intelligence is seen in empirical life as present in such varied things as the skillful military planning of an army general, the ingenious exploitation of a market situation by a business entrepreneur, effective methods of survival by a disadvantaged slum dweller, the clever meeting of the problems of his world by a peasant or a primitive tribesman, the cunning of low-grade delinquent-girl morons in a detention home, and the construction of telling verse by a poet. It should be immediately clear how ridiculous and unwarranted it is to believe that the operationalizing of intelligence through a given intelligence test yields a satisfactory picture of intelligence. To form an empirically satisfactory picture of intelligence, a picture that may be taken as having empirical validation, it is necessary to catch and study intelligence as it is in play in actual empirical life instead of relying on a specialized and usually arbitrary selection of one area of its presumed manifestation. This observation applies equally and fully to all instances of so-called operational procedures. If the concept or proposition that is being operationalized is taken to refer to something that is present in the empirical world, one cannot, as a true empirical scientist, escape the necessity of covering and studying representative forms of such empirical presense. To select (usually arbitrarily) some one form of empirical reference and to assume that the operationalized study of this one form catches the full empirical coverage of the concept or proposition is, of course, begging the question. It is this deficiency, a deficiency that runs so uniformly through operational procedure, that shows that operationalism falls far short of providing the empirical validation necessary to empirical science.

To summarize the foregoing discussion, the four customary means—adhering to scientific protocol, engaging in replication, testing hypotheses, and using operational procedure—do not provide the empirical validation that genuine empirical social science requires. They give no assurance that premises, problems, data, relations, concepts, and interpretations are empirically valid. Very simply put, the only way to get this assurance is to go directly to the empirical social world—to see through meticulous examination of it whether one's premises or root images of it, one's questions and problems posed for it, the data one chooses out of it, the concepts through which one sees and analyzes it, and the interpretations one applies to it are actually borne out. Current methodology gives no encouragement or sanction to such direct examination of the empirical social world. Thus, a diligent effort, apart from the research study one undertakes, to see if the empirical area under study corresponds in fact to one's underlying images of it, is a rarity. Similarly, a careful independent examination of the empirical area to see if the problem one is posing represents meaningfully what is going on in that empirical area is scarcely done. Similarly, an independent careful examination of the empirical area to see if what one constructs as data are genuinely meaningful data in that empirical area is almost unheard of. Similarly, a careful identification of what one's concepts are supposed to refer to, and then an independent examination of the empirical area to see if its content sustains, rejects, or qualifies the concept, are far from being customary working practices. And so on. I do not believe that I misrepresent current social and psychological research by saying that the predominant procedure is to take for granted one's premises about the nature of the empirical world and not to examine those premises; to take one's problems as valid because they sound good or because they stem from some theoretical scheme; to cling to some model because it is elegant and logically tight; to regard as empirically valid the data one chooses because such data fit one's conception of the problem; to be satisfied

32

with the empirical relevance of one's concepts because they have a nice connotative ring or because they are current intellectual coins of the realm.

(3) It is no wonder that the broad arena of research inquiry in the social and psychological sciences has the character of a grand display and clash of social philosophies. Instead of going to the empirical social world in the first and last instances, resort is made instead to a priori theoretical schemes, to sets of unverified concepts, and to canonized protocols of research procedure. These come to be the governing agents in dealing with the empirical social world, forcing research to serve their character and bending the empirical world to their premises. If this indictment seems unwarranted I merely call attention to the following: the array of conflicting schemes as to the nature and composition of human society and the conspicuous ease with which the adherents of each scheme "validate" the scheme through their own research; the astonishing fact that the overwhelming proportion of key concepts have not been pinned down in their empirical reference in the proper sense that one can go to instances in the empirical world and say safely that this is an instance of the concept and that is not an instance (try this out with such representative concepts as mores, alienation, value, integration, socialization, need-disposition, power, and cultural deprivation); the innumerable instances of scholars designing and pursuing elegant schemes of research into areas of social life with which they have little if any familiarity; and an endless parade of research studies that consist of no more than applying an already devised instrument, such as a scale or test, to a different setting of group life. Without wishing to be overly harsh, I believe one must recognize that the prevailing mode in the social and psychological sciences is to turn away from direct examination of the empirical social world and to give preference, instead, to theoretical schemes, to preconceived models, to arrays of vague concepts, to sophisticated techniques of research, and to an almost slavish adherence to what passes as the proper protocol of research inquiry. The fact that such theories, such models, such concepts, such techniques, and such a scientific protocol are brought to bear on the empirical world means little in itself. If the application were done systematically to test the empirical validity of the theory, the model, the concept, the technique, and the scientific protocol, all would be well. But this is

not the order of the day. The prevailing disposition and practice is to allow the theory, the model, the concept, the technique, and the scientific protocol to coerce the research and thus to bend the resulting analytical depictions of the empirical world to suit their form. In this sense, much current scientific inquiry in the social and psychological sciences is actually social philosophizing.

I repeat once more that what is needed is to gain empirical validation of the premises, the problems, the data, their lines of connection, the concepts, and the interpretations involved in the act of scientific inquiry. The road to such empirical validation does not lie in the manipulation of the method of inquiry; it lies in the examination of the empirical social world. It is not to be achieved by formulating and elaborating catchy theories, by devising ingenious models, by seeking to emulate the advanced procedures of the physical sciences, by adopting the newest mathematical and statistical schemes, by coining new concepts, by developing more precise quantitative techniques, or by insisting on adherence to the canons of research design. Such preoccupations, without prejudice to their merit in other respects, are just not headed in the direction that is called for here. What is needed is a return to the empirical social world.

A call for direct examination of the empirical social world is not likely to make any sense to most social scientists. They would say that this is exactly what they are doing in their research. They would hold that they are examining the empirical world directly when they do such things as collect and analyze various kinds of census data, make social surveys, secure declarations from people through questionnaires, use polls, undertake discriminating clinical examination, employ scales and refined measuring instruments, bring social action into controlled laboratory situations, undertake careful computer simulation of social life, and use crucial empirical data to test hypotheses. They would go further and say in a spirit of righteous indignation that not only do they examine the empirical social world directly but that they examine it in the only allowable proper manner—by adhering rigorously to the canons of long-tested scientific procedure. Thus, in place of the loose, vague, and impressionistic accounts that come from laymen and journalists they provide precise and tested empirical data, focused in a decisive way on given problems and enabling the isolation of clean-cut relations. This view, that in following established scientific protocol they are engaging in direct examination of the empirical social world, is deeply entrenched among social scientists. For this reason I find it necessary to make clear what I mean by the exhortation to turn to a direct examination of the empirical social world.

Let me begin by identifying the empirical social world in the case of human beings. This world is the actual group life of human beings. It consists of what they experience and do, individually and collectively, as they engage in their respective forms of living; it covers the large complexes of interlaced activities that grow up as the actions of some spread out to affect the actions of others; and it embodies the large variety of relations between the participants. This empirical world is evidenced, to take a few examples, by what is happening in the life of a boy's gang, or among the top management of an industrial corporation, or in militant racial groups, or among the police confronted by such groups, or among the young people in a country, or among the Catholic clergy, or in the experience of individuals in their different walks of life. The empirical social world, in short, is the world of everyday experience, the top layers of which we see in our lives and recognize in the lives of others. The life of a human society, or of any segment of it, or of any organization in it, or of its participants consists of the action and experience of people as they meet the situations that arise in their respective worlds. The problems of the social and psychological sciences necessarily arise out of, and go back to, this body of ongoing group life. This is true whether the problems refer to what is immediately taking place, as in the case of a student riot, or to the background causes of such a riot, or to the organization of institutions, or to the stratified relations of people, or to the ways in which people guide their lives, or to the personal organization of individuals formed through participation in group life. Ongoing group life, whether in the past or the present, whether in the case of this or that people, whether in one or another geographical area, is the empirical social world of the social and psychological sciences.

Several simple yet highly important observations need to be made with regard to the study of this world. The first is that almost by definition the research scholar does not have a firsthand acquaintance with the sphere of social life that he proposes to study. He is rarely a participant in that sphere and usually is not in close touch with the actions and the experiences of the people who are involved in that sphere. His position is almost always that of an outsider; as such he is markedly limited in simple knowledge of what takes place in the given sphere of life. This is no accusation against research scholars; it is a simple observation that applies to all human beings in their relation to an area of life that they do not know closely through personal association. The sociologist who proposes to study crime, or student unrest in Latin America, or political elites in Africa, and the psychologist who undertakes to study adolescent drug use, or aspirations among Negro school children, or social judgments among delinquents exemplify this almost inevitable absence of intimate acquaintance with the area of life under consideration. The initial position of the social scientist and the psychologist is practically always one of lack of familiarity with what is actually taking place in the sphere of life chosen for study.

This leads me to a second simple observation, namely, that despite this lack of firsthand acquaintance the research scholar will unwittingly form some kind of a picture of the area of life he proposes to study. He will bring into play the beliefs and images that he already has to fashion a more or less intelligible view of the area of life. In this respect he is like all human beings. Whether we be laymen or scholars, we necessarily view any unfamiliar area of group life through images we already possess. We may have no firsthand acquaintance with life among delinquent groups, or in labor unions, or in legislative committees, or among bank executives, or in a religious cult, yet given a few cues we readily form serviceable pictures of such life. This, as we all know, is the point at which stereotyped images enter and take control. All of us, as scholars, have our share of common stereotypes that we use to see a sphere of empirical social life that we do not know. In addition, the research scholar in the social sciences has another set of pre-established images that he uses. These images are constituted by his theories, by the beliefs current in his own professional circles, and by his ideas of how the empirical world must be set up to allow him to follow his research procedure. No careful observer can honestly deny that this is true. We see it clearly in the shaping of pictures of the empirical world to fit one's theories, in the organizing of such pictures in terms of the concepts and beliefs that enjoy current acceptance among one's set of colleagues, and in the molding of such pictures to fit the demands of scientific protocol. We must say in all honesty that the research scholar in the social sciences who undertakes to study a given sphere of social life that he does not know at first hand will fashion a picture of that sphere in terms of pre-established images.

There is no quarrel with this natural disposition and practice if the given research inquiry is guided by a conscientious and continuous effort to test and revise one's images, but this is not the prevailing motif in present-day social and psychological science. Theoretical positions are held tenaciously, the concepts and beliefs in one's field are gratuitously accepted as inherently true, and the canons of scientific procedure are sacrosanct. It is not surprising, consequently, that the images that stem from these sources control the inquiry and shape the picture of the sphere of life under study. In place of being tested and modified by firsthand acquaintance with the sphere of life they become a *substitute* for such acquaintance. Since this is a serious charge let me explain it.

To begin with, most research inquiry (certainly research inquiry modeled in terms of current methodology) is not designed to develop a close and reasonably full familiarity with the area of life under study. There is no demand on the research scholar to do a lot of free exploration in the area, getting close to the people involved in it, seeing it in a variety of situations they meet, noting their problems and observing how they handle them, being party to their conversations, and watching their life as it flows along. In place of such exploration and flexible pursuit of intimate contact with what is going on, reliance is put on starting with a theory or model, posing a problem in terms of the model, setting a hypothesis with regard to the problem, outlining a mode of inquiry to test that hypothesis, using standardized instruments to get precise data, and so forth. I merely wish to reassert here that current designs of "proper" research procedure do not encourage or provide for the development of firsthand acquaintance with the sphere of life under study.* Moreover, the scholar who lacks that firsthand familiarity is highly unlikely to recognize that he is missing anything. Not being aware

---

* See how far one gets in submitting proposals for exploratory studies to fund-granting agencies with their professional boards of consultants, or as doctoral dissertations in our advanced graduate departments of sociology and psychology! Witness the barrage of questions that arise: Where is your research design? What is your model? What is your guiding hypothesis? How are you operationalizing the hypothesis? What are your independent and dependent variables? What standard instruments are you going to use to get the data for your variables? What is your sample? What is your control group? And so on. Such questions presume in advance that the student has the firsthand knowledge that the exploratory study seeks to secure. Since he doesn't have it the protocolized research procedure becomes the substitute for getting it!

of the knowledge that would come from firsthand acquaintance, he does not know that he is missing that knowledge. Since the sanctioned scheme of scientific inquiry is taken for granted as the correct means of treatment and analysis, he feels no need to be concerned with firsthand familiarity with that sphere of life. In this way, the established protocol of scientific inquiry becomes the unwitting substitute for a direct examination of the empirical social world. The questions that are asked, the problems that are set, the leads that are followed, the kinds of data that are sought, the relations that are envisioned, and the kinds of interpretations that are striven toward—all these stem from the scheme of research inquiry instead of from familiarity with the empirical area under study.

There can be no question that the substitution of which I write takes place. The logical question that arises is, "So what?" Why is it important or necessary to have a firsthand knowledge of the area of social life under study? One would quickly dismiss this as a silly question were it not implied so extensively and profoundly in the social and psychological research of our time.* So the question should be faced. The answer to it is simply that the empirical social world consists of ongoing group life and one has to get close to this life to know what is going on in it. If one is going to respect the social world, one's problems, guiding conceptions, data, schemes of relationship, and ideas of interpretation have to be faithful to that empirical world. This is especially true in the case of human group life because of the persistent tendency of human beings in their collective life to build up separate worlds, marked by an operating milieu of different life situations and by the possession of different beliefs and conceptions for handling these situations. One merely has to think of the different worlds in the case of a military elite, the clergy of a church, modern city prostitutes, a peasant revolutionary body, professional politicians, slum dwellers, the directing management of a large industrial corporation, a gambling syndicate, a uni-

* Kudos in our fields today is gained primarily by devising a striking theory, or elaborating a grand theoretical system, or proposing a catchy scheme of analysis, or constructing a logically neat or elegant model, or cultivating and developing advanced statistical and mathematical techniques, or executing studies that are gems of research design, or (to mention something I am not treating in this essay) engaging in brilliant speculative analysis of what is happening in some area of social life. To study through firsthand observation what is actually happening in a given area of social life is given a subsidiary or peripheral position—it is spoken of as "soft" science or journalism.

versity faculty, and so on endlessly. The modes of living of such groups, the parade of situations they must handle, their institutions and their organizations, the relations between their members, the views and images through which they see their worlds, the personal organizations formed by their members—all these and more reflect their different empirical worlds. One should not blind oneself to a recognition of the fact that human beings in carrying on their collective life form very different kinds of worlds. To study them intelligently one has to know these worlds, and to know the worlds one has to examine them closely. No theorizing, however ingenious, and no observance of scientific protocol, however meticulous, are substitutes for developing a familiarity with what is actually going on in the sphere of life under study.

We should add that ongoing group life, whether in its entirety or in any of its spheres, takes place, as far as our perceptions of it are concerned, on different levels. The person who perceives nothing of it can know essentially nothing of it. The person who perceives it at a great distance, seeing just a little bit of it, can have correspondingly only a limited knowledge of it. The person who participates in it will have a greater knowledge of it, although if he is a naïve and unobservant participant his knowledge may be very restricted and inaccurate. The participant who is very observant will have fuller and more accurate knowledge. But there are levels of happening that are hidden to all participants. If we view the process of ongoing group life in this way, as I believe we are compelled to do, the study of such group life requires us to expand and deepen our perception of it. This is the direction of movement if we wish to form an accurate knowledge of it—movement from ignorance or an uninformed position to greater and more accurate awareness of what is taking place. The metaphor that I like is that of lifting the veils that obscure or hide what is going on. The task of scientific study is to lift the veils that cover the area of group life that one proposes to study. The veils are not lifted by substituting, in whatever degree, preformed images for firsthand knowledge. The veils are lifted by getting close to the area and by digging deep into it through careful study. Schemes of methodology that do not encourage or allow this betray the cardinal principle of respecting the nature of one's empirical world.

How does one get close to the empirical social world and dig deeply into it? This is not a simple matter of just approaching a given area and looking at it. It is a tough job requiring a high order of careful and honest probing, creative yet disciplined imagination, resourcefulness and flexibility in study, pondering over what one is finding, and a constant readiness to test and recast one's views and images of the area. It is exemplified among the grand figures of the natural sciences by Charles Darwin. It is not "soft" study merely because it does not use quantitative procedure or follow a premapped scientific protocol. That it is demanding in a genuinely rigorous sense can be seen in the analysis of its two fundamental parts. I term these parts respectively as "exploration" and "inspection." These two modes of inquiry clearly distinguish the direct naturalistic examination of the empirical social world from the mode of inquiry espoused by current methodology. I wish to sketch what is involved in exploration and inspection.

EXPLORATION. Exploratory study of human group life is the means of achieving simultaneously two complementary and inter-knit objectives. On the one hand, it is the way by which a research scholar can form a close and comprehensive acquaintance with a sphere of social life that is unfamiliar and hence unknown to him. On the other hand, it is the means of developing and sharpening his inquiry so that his problem, his directions of inquiry, data, analytical relations, and interpretations arise out of, and remain grounded in, the empirical life under study. Exploration is by definition a flexible procedure in which the scholar shifts from one to another line of inquiry, adopts new points of observation as his study progresses, moves in new directions previously unthought of, and changes his recognition of what are relevant data as he acquires more information and better understanding. In these respects, exploratory study stands in contrast to the prescribed and circumscribed procedure demanded by current scientific protocol. The flexibility of exploratory procedure does not mean that there is no direction to the inquiry; it means that the focus is originally broad but becomes progressively sharpened as the inquiry proceeds. The purpose of exploratory investigation is to move toward a clearer understanding of how one's problem is to be posed, to learn what are the appropriate data, to develop ideas of what are significant lines of relation, and to evolve one's conceptual tools in the light of what one is learning about the area of life. In this respect it differs from the somewhat pretentious posture of the research scholar who under established scientific protocol is required in advance of his study to present a fixed and clearly structured problem, to know what kinds of data he is to collect, to have and hold to a prearranged set of techniques, and to shape his findings by previously established categories.

Because of its flexible nature, exploratory inquiry is not pinned down to any particular set of techniques. Its guiding maxim is to use any ethically allowable procedure that offers a likely possibility of getting a clearer picture of what is going on in the area of social life. Thus, it may involve direct observation, interviewing of people, listening to their conversations, securing life-history accounts, using letters and diaries, consulting public records, arranging for group discussions, and making counts of an item if this appears worthwhile. There is no protocol to be followed in the use of any one of these procedures; the procedure should be adapted to its circumstances and guided by judgment of its propriety and fruitfulness. Yet a few special points should be borne in mind in such exploratory research. One should sedulously seek participants in the sphere of life who are acute observers and who are well informed. One such person is worth a hundred others who are merely unobservant participants. A small number of such individuals, brought together as a discussion and resource group, is more valuable many times over than any representative sample. Such a group, discussing collectively their sphere of life and probing into it as they meet one another's disagreements, will do more to lift the veils covering the sphere of life than any other device that I know of.

It is particularly important in exploratory research for the scholar to be constantly alert to the need of testing and revising his images, beliefs, and conceptions of the area of life he is studying. Part of such testing and revision will come from direct observation and from what informants tell him, but since his task extends to a probing into areas beneath those known to his informants, he should cultivate assiduously a readiness to view his area of study in new ways. Darwin, who is acknowledged as one of the world's greatest naturalistic observers on record, has noted the ease with which observation becomes and remains imprisoned by images. He recommends two ways of helping to break such captivity. One is to ask oneself all kinds of questions about what he is studying, even seemingly ludicrous questions. The posing of such questions helps to sensitize the observer to different and new perspectives. The other recommended procedure is to record all observations that challenge one's working conceptions as well as any observation that is odd and interesting even though its relevance is not immediately clear; Darwin has indicated from his personal experience how readily such observations disappear from memory and that, when retained and subjected to reflection, they usually are the pivots for a fruitful redirection of one's perspective.

The aim of exploratory research is to develop and fill out as comprehensive and accurate a picture of the area of study as conditions allow. The picture should enable the scholar to feel at home in the area, to talk from a basis of fact and not from speculation. The picture provides the scholar with a secure bearing so that he knows that the questions he asks of the empirical area are meaningful and relevant to it, that the problem he poses is not artificial, that the kinds of data he seeks are significant in terms of the empirical world, and that the leads he follows are faithful to its nature. Considering the crucial need and value of exploratory research in the case of the social and psychological sciences, it is an odd commentary on these sciences that their current methodological preoccupations are practically mute on this type of research.

It should be pointed out that the mere descriptive information unearthed through exploratory research may serve, in itself, to provide the answers to theoretical questions that the scholar may have in mind with regard to what he is studying. All too frequently, the scholar confronted with an unfamiliar area of social life will fabricate, in advance, analytical schemes that he believes necessary to account for the problematic features of the area. One of the interesting values of exploratory study is that the fuller descriptive account that it yields will frequently give an adequate explanation of what was problematic without the need of invoking any theory or proposing any analytical scheme. However, the picture of the sphere of social life that is formed through effective exploration does not terminate what is required by careful direct examination of the empirical social world. Such direct examination sets the need for another procedure that I find it convenient to label "inspection."

INSPECTION. The direct examination of the empirical social world is not limited to the construction of comprehensive and intimate accounts of what takes place. It should also embody analysis. The

42

research scholar who engages in direct examination should aim at casting his problem in a theoretical form, at unearthing generic relations, at sharpening the connotative reference of his concepts, and at formulating theoretical propositions. Such analysis is the proper aim of empirical science, as distinguished from the preparation of mere descriptive accounts. How is scientific analysis to be undertaken in the *direct* examination of the empirical social world, especially in the case of the account of that world yielded by exploration? The common answer is to apply to that account the scheme of scientific analysis espoused in current methodology. This scheme has the following form: Start with a theory or model that is framed in terms of relations between concepts or categories; use the theory to set up a specific problem in the area under study; convert the problem into specific kinds of independent and dependent variables that represent concepts or categories; employ precise techniques to get the data; discover the relations between the variables; and use the theory and model to explain these relations. To apply this conventional scheme to the account yielded by exploration would certainly be a gain over what is usually done, in that one would be working with data derived from what is actually happening rather than from what one imagines to be happening. Yet, in my judgment, this conventional protocol of scientific analysis is not suitable or satisfactory for the kind of analysis that is needed in direct examination of the empirical social world. Even though using the more realistic data yielded by exploration, the conventional protocol of scientific analysis still forces such data into an artificial framework that seriously limits and impairs genuine empirical analysis. Scientific analysis requires two things: clear, discriminating analytical elements and the isolation of relations between these elements. The conventional protocol does not pin down in an exact way the nature of the analytical elements in the empirical social world nor does it ferret out in an exacting manner the relation between these analytical elements. A different analytical procedure is necessary. I think that "inspection" constitutes this necessary procedure.

By "inspection" I mean an intensive focused examination of the empirical content of whatever analytical elements are used for purposes of analysis, and this same kind of examination of the empirical nature of the relations between such elements. Let me explain this abstract statement. By analytical elements I have in mind whatever general or categorical items are employed as the key items in the analysis, such as integration, social mobility, assimilation, charismatic leadership, bureaucratic relation, authority system, suppression of dissent, morale, relative deprivation, attitudes, and institutional commitment. As the examples suggest, such analytical elements may refer to processes, organization, relations, networks of relations, states of being, elements of personal organization, and happenings. These analytical elements may be cast in differing degrees of generality, ranging from something very broad such as integration to something more restricted such as mobility aspiration in the case of urban Negro adolescents. The procedure of inspection is to subject such analytical elements to meticulous examination by careful flexible scrutiny of the empirical instances covered by the analytical element. The empirical instances are those that appear in the area under study; their careful flexible scrutiny is done in the context of the empirical area in which they take place. Thus in the case of an analytical element such as assimilation, referring let us say to the assimilation of girls into organized prostitution, the empirical instances would consist, of course, of the separate careers of girls undergoing the assimilation. The careful scrutiny of such instances with an eye to disengaging the generic nature of such assimilation represents what I have in mind by "inspection."

As a procedure, inspection consists of examining the given analytical element by approaching it in a variety of different ways, viewing it from different angles, asking many different questions of it, and returning to its scrutiny from the standpoint of such questions. The prototype of inspection is represented by our handling of a strange physical object; we may pick it up, look at it closely, turn it over as we view it, look at it from this or that angle, raise questions as to what it might be, go back and handle it again in the light of our questions, try it out, and test it in one way or another. This close shifting scrutiny is the essence of inspection. Such inspection is not preset, routinized, or prescribed; it only becomes such when we already know what it is and thus can resort to a specific test, as in the case of a technician. Instead, inspection is flexible, imaginative, creative, and free to take new directions. This type of examination can be done also in the case of a social object, or a process, or a relationship, or any one of the elements used in the theoretical analysis of a given area or aspect of empirical social life. One goes to the empirical instances of the analytical element, views them in their different concrete settings, looks at them from different positions, asks questions of them with regard to their generic character, goes back and re-examines them, compares them with one another, and in this manner sifts out the nature of the analytical element that the empirical instances represent. This pinning down of the nature of the analytical element is done through scrutiny of the empirical life itself, by discovering what that empirical life yields when subjected to such a careful, flexible probing. I know of no other way to determine the nature of an analytical element that one proposes to use in the analysis of a given empirical area of social life and still be sure that the analytical element is both germane and valid for such use.

It should be clear that inspection as a mode of inquiry is the antithesis of scientific inquiry as outlined in current methodology in the social and psychological sciences. Inspection is not tied down to a fixed mode of approach and procedure; it does not start with analytical elements whose nature has been set in advance and never tested or revised in the course of their use; and it develops the nature of the analytical elements through the examination of the empirical world itself. Inspection is the opposite of giving a "nature" to the analytical element by operationalizing the element (for example, defining intelligence in terms of the intelligence quotient). It seeks, instead, to identify the nature of the analytical element by an intense scrutiny of its instances in the empirical world. Because of the failure to employ the procedure of inspection, the use of analytical elements in current social science research is somewhat scandalous. Nowhere is this more evident than in the state of our concepts, which in the last analysis are our analytical elements. The preponderant majority of our concepts are conspicuously vague and imprecise in their empirical connotation,* yet we use them right and left in our analyses, without concern about elaborating, refining, or testing their empirical connotation. The needed improvement of

---

* In order that this charge not be left hanging in the air, the reader is invited to try to pin down the empirical meaning of the following representative array of commonly used social science concepts: mores, integration, social role, alienation, socialization, attitude, value, anomie, and deviance. Empirical meaning is not given by a definition that merely serves the purpose of discourse; it exists instead in a specification that allows one to go to the empirical world and to say securely in the case of any empirical thing that this is an instance of the concept and that is not. Let the reader try his hand at doing this with the above concepts in observing what happens around him.

their empirical meaning is not accomplished in any degree whatsoever by "operationalizing" the concepts. It can be done only by the careful inspection of their empirical instances, in the course of which one disengages and refines their character.

Inspection is also the appropriate procedure for carrying out the other part of social analysis—the isolation of relations between analytical elements. Such a relation presumes the existence of a meaningful connection between the components *in the empirical world*. As something so presumed, the relation stands in need of scrutiny in that world, just as much as is true of assertions about the empirical connotation of analytical elements. The asserted relation needs to be pinned down and tested by careful, flexible scrutiny of its empirical instances. Without this inspection one is captive to one's prior image or conception of the relation, without the benefit of knowing whether that conception is empirically valid and without the means of refining and improving the conception through a meticulous examination of empirical instances.

Exploration and inspection, representing respectively depiction and analysis, constitute the necessary procedure in direct examination of the empirical social world. They comprise what is sometimes spoken of as "naturalistic" investigation—investigation that is directed to a given empirical world in its natural, ongoing character instead of to a simulation of such a world, or to an abstraction from it (as in the case of laboratory experimentation), or to a substitute for the world in the form of a preset image of it. The merit of naturalistic study is that it respects and stays close to the empirical domain. This respect and closeness is particularly important in the social sciences because of the formation of different worlds and spheres of life by human beings in their group existence. Such worlds both represent and shape the social life of people, their activities, their relations, and their institutions. Such a world or sphere of life is almost always remote and unknown to the research scholar; this is a major reason why he wants to study it. To come to know it he should get close to it in its actual empirical character. Without doing this he has no assurance that his guiding imagery of the sphere or world, or the problem he sets forth for it, or the leads he lays down, or the data he selects, or the kinds of relations that he prefigures between them, or the theoretical views that guide his interpretations are empirically valid. Naturalistic inquiry, embracing the dual procedures of exploration and inspection, is clearly necessary in the scientific study of human group lif:. It qualifies as being "scientific" in the best meaning of that term.

My presentation has set forth rather sharply the opposition between naturalistic inquiry, in the form of exploration and inspection, and the formalized type of inquiry so vigorously espoused in current methodology. This opposition needs to be stressed in the hope of releasing social scientists from unwitting captivity to a format of inquiry that is taken for granted as the naturally proper way in which to conduct scientific study. The spokesmen for naturalistic inquiry in the social and psychological sciences today are indeed very few despite the fact that many noteworthy studies in the social sciences are products of naturalistic study. The consideration of naturalistic inquiry scarcely enters into the content of present-day methodology. Further, as far as I can observe, training in naturalistic inquiry is soft-pedaled or not given at all in our major graduate departments. There is a widespread ignorance of it and an accompanying blindness to its necessity. This is unfortunate for the social and psychological sciences since, as empirical sciences, their mission is to come to grips with their empirical world.

METHODOLOGICAL ORIENTATION

Symbolic interactionism is a down-to-earth approach to the scientific study of human group life and human conduct. Its empirical world is the natural world of such group life and conduct. It lodges its problems in this natural world, conducts its studies in it, and derives its interpretations from such naturalistic studies. If it wishes to study religious cult behavior it will go to actual religious cults and observe them carefully as they carry on their lives. If it wishes to study social movements it will trace carefully the career, the history, and the life experiences of actual movements. If it wishes to study drug use among adolescents it will go to the actual life of such adolescents to observe and analyze such use. And similarly with respect to other matters that engage its attention. Its methodological stance, accordingly, is that of direct examination of the empirical social world—the methodological approach that I have discussed above. It recognizes that such direct examination permits the scholar to meet all of the basic requirements of an empirical science: to confront an empirical world that is available for observation and analysis; to raise abstract problems with regard to that world; to gather necessary data through careful and disciplined examination of that world; to unearth relations between categories of such data; to formulate propositions with regard to such relations; to weave such propositions into a theoretical scheme; and to test the problems, the data, the relations, the propositions, and the theory by renewed examination of the empirical world. Symbolic interactionism is not misled by the mythical belief that to be scientific it is necessary to shape one's study to fit a pre-established protocol of empirical inquiry, such as adopting the working procedure of advanced physical science, or devising in advance a fixed logical or mathematical model, or forcing the study into the mould of laboratory experimentation, or imposing a statistical or mathematical framework on the study, or organizing it in terms of preset variables, or restricting it to a particular standardized procedure such as survey research. Symbolic interactionism recognizes that the genuine mark of an empirical science is to respect the nature of its empirical world—to fit its problems, its guiding conceptions, its procedures of inquiry, its techniques of study, its concepts, and its theories to that world. It believes that this determination of problems, concepts, research techniques, and theoretical schemes should be done by the *direct* examination of the actual empirical social world rather than by working with a simulation of that world, or with a preset model of that world, or with a picture of that world derived from a few scattered observations of it, or with a picture of that world fashioned in advance to meet the dictates of some imported theoretical scheme or of some scheme of "scientific" procedure, or with a picture of the world built up from partial and untested accounts of that world. For symbolic interactionism the nature of the empirical social world is to be discovered, to be dug out by a direct, careful, and probing examination of that world.

This methodological stance provides the answer to the frequent charge that symbolic interactionism does not lend itself to scientific research. This is an astonishing charge. It is evident that those who advance it are using the ideas of scientific inquiry in current methodology as the standard for judging symbolic interactionism.

They ask, for example, how would the symbolic interactionist "operationalize" the "self," or devise an appropriate scale to measure the interpretation of gestures, or set up a controlled experiment on the process of developing new self-conceptions, or use statistical procedures in analyzing the formation of new social objects, or bring the "generalized other" inside the framework of such procedures as stochastic analysis, systems analysis, or operational research. Such demands are non-sensical (although some symbolic interactionists take them seriously and try to meet them!). The demands show a profound misunderstanding of both scientific inquiry and symbolic interactionism. The concepts and propositions of symbolic interactionism are devised for the direct examination of the empirical social world. Their value and their validity are to be determined in that examination and not in seeing how they fare when subjected to the alien criteria of an irrelevant methodology.

Certainly, the basic premises of symbolic interactionism—what I have discussed earlier as its root images—have to have their empirical validity tested. If they cannot survive that test they, together with the scheme of symbolic interactionism which they undergird, should be thrown ruthlessly aside. (This same test should be made in the case of any and every other scheme proposed for the study and analysis of human society and conduct.) The manner of testing the premises is to go to the empirical social world since the premises are declarations of the nature of that world. Let me remind the reader of the basic premises of symbolic interactionism: human group life consists of the fitting to each other of the lines of action of the participants; such aligning of actions takes place predominantly by the participants indicating to one another what to do and in turn interpreting such indications made by the others; out of such interaction people form the objects that constitute their worlds; people are prepared to act toward their objects on the basis of the meaning these objects have for them; human beings face their world as organisms with selves, thus allowing each to make indications to himself; human action is constructed by the actor on the basis of what he notes, interprets, and assesses; and the interlinking of such ongoing action constitutes organizations, institutions, and vast complexes of interdependent relations. To test the validity of these premises one must go to a direct examination of actual human group life—not to a contrived laboratory setting, not to a scheme of operationalizing concepts, not to a testing of hypotheses, and not to a scrutiny of whether the premises can be made to fit a protocol of research procedure. The premises of symbolic interactionism are simple. I think they can be readily tested and validated merely by observing what goes on in social life under one's nose. I would like, somewhat contentiously, to invite social scientists to undertake this same kind of test of the premises underlying other schemes for the study of human society and social action that are in vogue today.

Granted that human group life has the character that is stated by the premises of symbolic interactionism, the general topic I wish to consider is how does one study human group life and social action. I do not have in mind an identification and analysis of the numerous separate procedures that may be employed at one or another point in carrying on exploration and inspection. There is a sizeable literature, very uneven to be true, on a fair number of such separate procedures, such as direct observation, field study, participant observation, case study, interviewing, use of life histories, use of letters and diaries, use of public documents, panel discussions, and use of conversations. There is great need, I may add, of careful circumspective study of such procedures, not to bring them inside a standardized format but to improve their capacity as instruments for discovering what is taking place in actual group life. My current concern, however, lies in a different direction, namely, to point out several of the more important methodological implications of the symbolic interactionist's view of human group life and social action. I want to consider such implications in the case of each of four central conceptions in symbolic interactionism. These four central conceptions are: (1) people, individually and collectively, are prepared to act on the basis of the meanings of the objects that comprise their world; (2) the association of people is necessarily in the form of a process in which they are making indications to one another and interpreting each other's indications; (3) social acts, whether individual or collective, are constructed through a process in which the actors note, interpret, and assess the situations confronting them; and (4) the complex interlinkages of acts that comprise organization, institutions, division of labor, and networks of interdependency are moving and not static affairs. I wish to discuss each of these in turn.

(1) The contention that people act on the basis of the meaning of their objects has profound methodological implications. It signifies

immediately that if the scholar wishes to understand the action of people it is necessary for him to see their objects as they see them. Failure to see their objects as they see them, or a substitution of his meanings of the objects for their meanings, is the gravest kind of error that the social scientist can commit. It leads to the setting up of a fictitious world. Simply put, people act toward things on the basis of the meaning that these things have for them, not on the basis of the meaning that these things have for the outside scholar. Yet we are confronted right and left with studies of human group life and of the behavior of people in which the scholar has made no attempt to find out how the people see what they are acting toward. This neglect is officially fostered by two pernicious tendencies in current methodology: (1) the belief that mere expertise in the use of scientific techniques plus facility in some given theory are sufficient equipment to study an unfamiliar area; and (2) the stress that is placed on being objective, which all too frequently merely means seeing things from the position of the detached outside observer. We have multitudes of studies of groups such as delinquents, police, military elites, restless students, racial minorities, and labor unions in which the scholar is unfamiliar with the life of the groups and makes little, if any, effort to get inside their worlds of meanings. We are compelled, I believe, to recognize that this is a widespread practice in the social sciences.

To try to identify the objects that comprise the world of an individual or a collectivity is not simple or easy for the scholar who is not familiar with that world. It requires, first of all, ability to place oneself in the position of the individual or collectivity. This ability to take the roles of others, like any other potential skill, requires cultivation to be effective. By and large, the training of scholars in the social sciences today is not concerned with the cultivation of this ability nor do their usual practices in research study foster its development. Second, to identify the objects of central concern one must have a body of relevant observations. These necessary observations are rarely those that are yielded by standard research procedure such as questionnaires, polls, scales, use of survey research items, or the setting of predesignated variables. Instead, they are in the form of descriptive accounts from the actors of how they see the objects, how they have acted toward the objects in a variety of different situations, and how they refer to the objects in their conversations with members of their own group. The depiction of key objects that emerge from such accounts should, in turn, be subject to probing and critical collective discussion by a group of well-informed participants in the given world. This latter procedure is a genuine "must" to guard against the admitted deficiencies of individual accounts. Third, as mentioned in earlier discussion, research scholars, like human beings in general, are slaves to their own pre-established images and thus are prone to assume that other people see the given objects as they, the scholars, see them. Scholars need to guard against this proneness and to give high priority to deliberate testing of their images.

All these observations make clear the need for a different methodological approach if one takes seriously the proposition that people act toward objects on the basis of the meaning of such objects for them. This proposition calls for kinds of inquiry significantly different from those generally sanctioned and encouraged today. Since people everywhere and in all of their groups live in worlds of objects and act in terms of the meaning of these objects to them, it is a matter of simple sense that one has to identify the objects and their meaning. The research position of symbolic interaction is predicated on this recognition.

(2) Symbolic interactionism sees group life as a process in which people, as they meet in their different situations, indicate lines of action to each other and interpret the indications made by others. This means, obviously, that their respective lines of behavior have to be built up in the light of the lines of action of the others with whom they are interacting. This adjustment of developing acts to each other takes place not merely between individuals in face-to-face association but also between collectivities such as industrial corporations or nations who have to deal with one another, and occurs also in the case of any one of us who gives consideration to the judgment of an outside audience or community in guiding his line of action. This need of adjusting to the lines of action of others is so evident in the simplest observations that I find it difficult to understand why it is so generally ignored or dismissed by social scientists.

The methodological implications of the premise are very telling. First of all, it raises the most serious question about the validity of most of the major approaches to the study and analysis of human group life that are followed today—approaches that treat social interaction as merely the medium through which determining factors produce behavior. Thus, sociologists ascribe behavior to such factors as social role, status, cultural prescription, norms, values, reference group affiliation, and mechanisms of societal equilibrium; and psychologists attribute behavior to such factors as stimuli configurations, organic drives, need-dispositions, emotions, attitudes, ideas, conscious motives, unconscious motives, and mechanisms of personal organization. Social interaction is treated as merely the arena in which these kinds of determining factors work themselves out into human action. These approaches grossly ignore the fact that social interaction is a formative process in its own right—that people in interaction are not merely giving expression to such determining factors in forming their respective lines of action but are directing, checking, bending, and transforming their lines of action in the light of what they encounter in the actions of others. In setting up studies of human group life and social action there is need to take social interaction seriously. It is necessary to view the given sphere of life under study as a moving process in which the participants are defining and interpreting each other's acts. It is important to see how this process of designation and interpretation is sustaining, undercutting, redirecting, and transforming the ways in which the participants are fitting together their lines of action. Such a necessary type of study cannot be done if it operates with the premise that group life is but the result of determining factors working through the interaction of people. Further, approaches organized on this latter premise are not equipped to study the process of social interaction. A different perspective, a different set of categories, and a different procedure of inquiry are necessary.

A second important methodological implication that comes from seeing that human interaction is a process of designation and interpretation is the lack of warrant for compressing the process of social interaction into any special form. Such compression is an outstanding vice in social science, both past and present. We see it exemplified in the quaint notion that social interaction is a process of developing "complimentary expectations"—a notion given wide currency by Talcott Parsons and serving as the basis of his scheme of human society as a harmoniously disposed social system. We see it illustrated, also, in the contrary premise that human society is organized basically in terms of a conflict process. We see it, still further, in the current popular view that human interaction follows the principles of "game theory." Anyone who observes social interaction with open eyes should readily recognize that human participants, both individually and collectively, meet each other's actions in diverse and varying forms. Sometimes they cooperate, sometimes they conflict with each other, sometimes they are tolerant of each other, sometimes they are indifferent to each other, sometimes they follow rigid rules in their interaction, and sometimes they engage in a free play of expressive behavior toward one another. To see all human interaction (and accordingly human society) as organized in the form of some special type of interaction does violence to the variety of forms that one can see if he wants to look. The very fact that human beings make indications to one another and interpret each other's indications in the light of the situation in which they are acting should make clear that the process of social interaction is not constrained to any single form. The task of the research scholar who is studying any sphere of social life is to ascertain what form of interaction is in play instead of imposing on that sphere some preset form of interaction. The identification of the kind of interaction that is in play is not achieved, except by chance, when the study itself presupposes a special form of interaction. A different investigating procedure is required. It is my experience that the interaction usually shifts back and forth from one to another form, depending on the situations that are being met by the interacting parties. Whatever be the case, the form of the social interaction is a matter for empirical discovery and not a matter to be fixed in advance.

(3) The view of social action held by symbolic interaction leads to a number of significant methodological consequences. Symbolic interactionism sees social action as consisting of the individual and collective activities of people who are engaged in social interaction —that is to say, activities whose own formation is made in the light of the activity of one another. Such activity makes up the ongoing social life of a human group, whether the group be small as a family or large as a nation. It is from the observation of social action that we derive the categories that we use to give conceptual order to the social makeup and social life of a human group—each one of such categories stands for a form or aspect of social action. Thus, a chief, a priest, a social role, a stratification arrangement, an institution, or a social process such as assimilation stands for a form or aspect of

social action; the category is meaningless unless seen and cast ultimately in terms of social action. In a valid sense social action is the
primary subject matter of social science, the subject matter from
which it starts and to which it must return with its schemes of analysis. Hence, an accurate picture and understanding of social action is
of crucial importance.

A part of this picture of social action as seen by symbolic interactionism has already been sketched in the immediately foregoing discussion of social interaction; that is, social action must be seen as
necessarily taking place within the process of social interaction.
The other part of the picture refers to the activity of the participant
in social interaction, whether the participant be an individual or a
collectivity. In other words, there is need to see social action in
terms of the actor since it is only actors who act. It is the position
of symbolic interactionism that the social action of the actor is *constructed* by him; it is not a mere release of activity brought about by
the play of initiating factors on his organization. In this sense, as
explained earlier, symbolic interactionism sees social action in a
markedly different way from that of current social and psychological
science. The actor (let me deal with the individual actor first) is
seen as one who is confronted with a situation in which he has to
act. In this situation, he notes, interprets, and assesses things with
which he has to deal in order to act. He can do this by virtue of
being able to interact or communicate with himself. Through such
self-interaction he constructs his line of action, noting what he wants
or what is demanded of him, setting up a goal, judging the possibilities of the situation, and prefiguring his line of action. In such self-
interaction he may hold his prospective act in suspension, abandon it,
check it at one or another point, revise it, or devise a substitute for it.
Symbolic interactionism declares that this is the way in which the
human being engages in his social action. Social scientists and
psychologists are invited, indeed beseeched, to observe their own
social action and see if this is not true. The human being is not a
mere responding organism, only responding to the play of factors
from his world or from himself; he is an acting organism who has to
cope with and handle such factors and who, in so doing, has to forge
and direct his line of action. As I have said earlier, he may do a
poor job in constructing his act, but construct it he must.

The same sort of picture exists in the case of the social action of a collectivity, such as a business corporation, a labor union, an army, a church, a boy's gang, or a nation. The difference is that the collectivity has a directing group or individual who is empowered to assess the operating situation, to note different things that have to be dealt with, and to map out a line of action. The self-interaction of a collectivity is in the form of discussion, counseling, and debate. The collectivity is in the same position as the individual in having to cope with a situation, in having to interpret and analyze the situation, and in having to construct a line of action.

The premise that social action is built up by the acting unit through a process of noting, interpreting, and assessing things and of mapping out a prospective line of action implies a great deal as to how social action should be studied. Basically put, it means that in order to treat and analyze social action one has to observe the process by which it is constructed. This, of course, is not done and cannot be done by any scheme that relies on the premise that social action is merely a product of pre-existing factors that play on the acting unit. A different methodological stance is called for. As opposed to an approach that sees social action as a product and then seeks to identify the determining or causative factors of such action, the required approach is to see the acting unit as confronted with an operating situation that it has to handle and vis-à-vis which it has to work out a line of action. The acting unit is lifted out of a position of being a neutral medium for the play of determining factors and is given the status of an active organizer of its action. This different stance means that the research scholar who is concerned with the social action of a given individual or group, or with a given type of social action, must see that action from the position of whoever is forming the action. He should trace the formation of the action in the way in which it is actually formed. This means seeing the situation as it is seen by the actor, observing what the actor takes into account, observing how he interprets what is taken into account, noting the alternative kinds of acts that are mapped out in advance, and seeking to follow the interpretation that led to the selection and execution of one of these prefigured acts. Such an identification and analysis of the career of the act is essential to an empirical understanding of social action—whether it be juvenile delinquency, suicide, revolutionary behavior, the behavior of Negro militants, the behavior of right-wing reactionary groups, or what not.

The reluctance, and indeed the failure, of social scientists and psychologists to pay attention to the formation of social action by the acting unit is astonishing in view of the fact that such formation is what actually goes on in empirical social life. This failure is an interesting example of scholars being committed to a collective view, in this instance a view that sees social action as product and that jumps to antecedent factors as explanatory causes.* The methodological position of symbolic interactionism is that social action must be studied in terms of how it is formed; its formation is a very different matter from the antecedent conditions that are taken as the "causes" of the social action and is not covered by any specification of such causes.

(4) Finally, I want to say something about the methodological consequences of the way in which symbolic interactionism looks upon the large or so-called molar parts or aspects of human society. These large parts or aspects constitute what have been traditionally the major objects of sociological interest—institutions, stratification arrangements, class systems, divisions of labor, large-scale corporate units and other big forms of societal organization. The tendency of sociologists is to regard these large complexes as entities operating in their own right with their own dynamics. Each is usually seen as a system, composed of given parts in interdependent arrangement and subject to the play of mechanisms that belong to the system as such. Structural functionalism, which is so popular today, is a good example (although only one example) of this view. Under the general view, the participants in the given unit of societal organization are logically merely media for the play and expression of the forces or mechanisms of the system itself; one turns to such

* In failing to see and trace the process of the formation of social action one can unwittingly make many serious errors. One example is that of grouping instances of social action in the same class because of their similar appearance as products and then reasoning that they must have common causes because of such similarity. This is done especially in one of the favorite preoccupations of many sociologists, that of studying "rates" of social behavior, such as the suicide rate, and then endeavoring to explain the given type of behavior by accounting for changes in its rate. The instances that enter into a rate of human behavior are instances of social action, every one of which has had a career of being formed by its respective actor. To bypass the study of this central process of formation and to assume that an explanation of the changes in a rate covers the process of formation is most gratuitous. A knowledge of the process of formation of the given instances would have very interesting consequences on one's picture of what the rate actually represents.

forces or mechanisms to account for what takes place. The given societal organization is likened to a huge machine or organism (I do not say this invidiously) in that its behavior and the behavior of its parts are to be explained in terms of the principles of operation of the societal organization itself.

Symbolic interactionism sees these large societal organizations or molar units in a different way. It sees them as arrangements of people who are interlinked in their respective actions. The organization and interdependency is between such actions of people stationed at different points. At any one point the participants are confronted by the organized activities of other people into which they have to fit their own acts. The concatenation of such actions taking place at the different points constitute the organization of the given molar unit or large-scale area. A skeletalized description of this organization would be the same for symbolic interactionism as for the other approaches. However, in seeing the organization as an organization of actions symbolic interactionism takes a different approach. Instead of accounting for the activity of the organization and its parts in terms of organizational principles or system principles, it seeks explanation in the way in which the participants define, interpret, and meet the situations at their respective points. The linking together of this knowledge of the concatenated actions yields a picture of the organized complex. Organizational principles or system principles may indeed identify the limits beyond which there could be no concatenation of actions, but they do not explain the form or nature of such concatenations. True, a given organization conceived from organizational principles may be imposed on a corporate unit or corporate area, as in the case of a reorganization of an army or an industrial system, but this represents the application of somebody's definition of what the organization should be. What happens in the wake of such application is something else, as we well know from striking examples in recent times. The point of view of symbolic interactionism is that large-scale organization has to be seen, studied, and explained in terms of the process of interpretation engaged in by the acting participants as they handle the situations at their respective positions in the organization. Such study, it may be noted, would throw a great deal of light on a host of matters of concern to the organizational theorist or to the system analyst—problems such as morale, the functioning of bureaucracy, blockage in effective communication, corruption and ranges of bribery, "exploiting the system," favoritism and cliquishness, the rise (and decline) of oligarchic control, the disintegration of the organization, or the infusion of new vigor into the organization. A knowledge of large-scale organizations and complexly organized areas is to be sought in the examination of the life of such organizations and areas as represented by what the participants do. This does not mean, as current phraseology would put it, turning from the molar to the minuscule; it means studying the molar in terms of its empirical character of being an interlinkage of action.

The shaping of inquiry to a study of what is done by the people comprising a complex organization or a complexly organized area sets no methodological problems for symbolic interactionism that are different from those discussed above. What is needed is the same type of exploratory and inspection procedure previously outlined. I would like to add, however, two noteworthy points that bear on the shift from seeing organization as a self-contained matter with its own principles to seeing it as an interlinkage of the activities of people.

One of these points refers to what I commented on earlier in indicating that stable and recurrent forms of joint action do not carry on automatically in their fixed form but have to be sustained by the meanings that people attach to the type of situation in which the joint action reoccurs. This observation applies to large-scale organization. Beneath the norms and rules that specify the type of action to be engaged in at any given point in the organizational complex there are two concurrent processes in which people are defining each other's perspectives and the individual, through self-interaction, is redefining his own perspective. What takes place in these two processes largely determines the status and the fate of the norms or rules; the rules may still be observed but the observance may be weak or hollow, or, contrariwise, reinforced or invested with greater vigor. Such shifts in the support of norms and rules are something other than applying sanctions or neglecting to apply them. They point to a separate area of happening in the interaction between people. Scholarly study or analysis of organization cannot afford to ignore the process of interaction between people that is responsible for sustaining organization as well as for affecting it in other ways.

The other point is a reminder of the need to recognize that joint action is temporally linked with previous joint action. One shuts a major door to the understanding of any form or instance of joint action if one ignores this connection. The application of this general point to the topic of large-scale societal organization is particularly in order. There is a noticeable neglect of this historical linkage by organizational theorists and system analysts in both their formulation of principles and their research. The complex organization or the complexly organized area is cut off by them, so to speak, from the background out of which it grew. This can only lead to misrepresentation. The designations and interpretations through which people form and maintain their organized relations are always in degree a carry-over from their past. To ignore this carry-over sets a genuine risk for the scholar. On this point the methodological posture of symbolic interactionism is to pay heed to the historical linkage of what is being studied.

CONCLUSION

My conclusion, in contrast to the undue length of this essay, is indeed brief. It can be expressed as a simple injunction: Respect the nature of the empirical world and organize a methodological stance to reflect that respect. This is what I think symbolic interactionism strives to do.

2

Sociological Implications of the Thought of George Herbert Mead

My purpose is to depict the nature of human society when seen from the point of view of George Herbert Mead. While Mead gave human society a position of paramount importance in his scheme of thought he did little to outline its character. His central concern was with cardinal problems of philosophy. The development of his ideas of human society was largely limited to handling these problems. His treatment took the form of showing that human group life was the essential condition for the emergence of consciousness, the mind, a world of objects, human beings as organisms possessing selves, and human conduct in the form of constructed acts. He reversed the traditional assumptions underlying philosophical, psychological, and sociological thought to the effect that human beings possess minds and consciousness as original "givens," that they live in worlds of pre-existing and self-constituted objects, that their behavior consists of responses to such objects, and that group life consists of the association of such reacting human organisms. In making his brilliant contributions along this line he did not map out a theoretical scheme of human society. However, such a scheme is implicit in his work. It has to be constructed by tracing the implica-

Reprinted from **The American Journal of Sociology** *by permission of The* **University of Chicago Press.**

tions of the central matters which he analyzed. This is what I propose to do. The central matters I shall consider are (1) the self, (2) the act, (3) social interaction, (4) objects, and (5) joint action.

THE SELF

Mead's picture of the human being as an actor differs radically from the conception of man that dominates current psychological and social science. He saw the human being as an organism having a self. The possession of a self converts the human being into a special kind of actor, transforms his relation to the world, and gives his action a unique character. In asserting that the human being has a self, Mead simply meant that the human being is an object to himself. The human being may perceive himself, have conceptions of himself, communicate with himself, and act toward himself. As these types of behavior imply, the human being may become the object of his own action. This gives him the means of interacting with himself—addressing himself, responding to the address, and addressing himself anew. Such self-interaction takes the form of making indications to himself and meeting these indications by making further indications. The human being can designate things to himself—his wants, his pains, his goals, objects around him, the presence of others, their actions, their expected actions, or whatnot. Through further interaction with himself, he may judge, analyze, and evaluate the things he has designated to himself. And by continuing to interact with himself he may plan and organize his action with regard to what he has designated and evaluated. In short, the possession of a self provides the human being with a mechanism of self-interaction with which to meet the world—a mechanism that is used in forming and guiding his conduct.

I wish to stress that Mead saw the self as a process and not as a structure. Here Mead clearly parts company with the great bulk of students who seek to bring a self into the human being by identifying it with some kind of organization or structure. All of us are familiar with this practice because it is all around us in the literature. Thus, we see scholars who identify the self with the "ego," or who regard the self as an organized body of needs or motives, or who think of it as an organization of attitudes, or who treat it as a structure of internalized norms and values. Such schemes which seek to lodge the self in a structure make no sense since they miss the reflexive process which alone can yield and constitute a self. For any posited structure to be a self, it would have to act upon and respond to itself—otherwise, it is merely an organization awaiting activation and release without exercising any effect on itself or on its operation. This marks the crucial weakness or inadequacy of the many schemes such as those referred to above, which misguidingly associate the self with some kind of psychological or personality structure. For example, the ego, as such, is not a self; it would be a self only by becoming reflexive, that is to say, acting toward or on itself. And the same thing is true of any other posited psychological structure. Yet, such reflexive action changes both the status and the character of the structure and elevates the process of self-interaction to the position of major importance.

We can see this in the case of the reflexive process that Mead has isolated in the human being. As mentioned, this reflexive process takes the form of the person making indications to himself, that is to say, noting things and determining their significance for his line of action. To indicate something is to stand over against it and to put oneself in the position of acting toward it instead of automatically responding to it. In the face of something which one indicates, one can withhold action toward it, inspect it, judge it, ascertain its meaning, determine its possibilities, and direct one's action with regard to it. With the mechanism of self-interaction the human being ceases to be a responding organism whose behavior is a product of what plays upon him from the outside, the inside, or both. Instead, he acts toward his world, interpreting what confronts him and organizing his action on the basis of the interpretation. To illustrate: a pain one identifies and interprets is very different from a mere organic feeling and lays the basis for doing something about it instead of merely responding organically to it; to note and interpret the activity of another person is very different from having a response released by that activity; to be aware that one is hungry is very different from merely being hungry; to perceive one's "ego" puts one in the position of doing something with regard to it instead of merely giving expression to the ego. As these illustrations show, the process of self-interaction puts the human being over against his world instead of merely in it, requires him to meet and handle his world through a defining process instead of merely responding to it, and forces him to construct his action instead of merely releasing it. This is the kind of acting organism that Mead sees man to be as a result of having a self.*

THE ACT

Human action acquires a radically different character as a result of being formed through a process of self-interaction. Action is built up in coping with the world instead of merely being released from a pre-existing psychological structure by factors playing on that structure. By making indications to himself and by interpreting what he indicates, the human being has to forge or piece together a line of action. In order to act the individual has to identify what he wants, establish an objective or goal, map out a prospective line of behavior, note and interpret the actions of others, size up his situation, check himself at this or that point, figure out what to do at other points, and frequently spur himself on in the face of dragging dispositions or discouraging settings. The fact that the human act is self-directed or built up means in no sense that the actor necessarily exercises excellence in its construction. Indeed, he may do a very poor job in constructing his act. He may fail to note things of which he should be aware, he may misinterpret things that he notes, he may exercise poor judgment, he may be faulty in mapping out prospective lines of conduct, and he may be half-hearted in contending with recalcitrant dispositions. Such deficiencies in the construction of his acts do not belie the fact that his acts are still constructed by him out of what he takes into account. What he takes into account are the things that he indicates to himself. They cover such matters as his wants, his feelings, his goals, the actions of others, the expectations and demands of others, the rules of his group, his situation, his conceptions of himself, his recollections, and his images of prospective lines of conduct. He is not in the mere recipient position of responding to such matters; he stands over against them and has to handle them.

* The self, or indeed human being, is not brought into the picture merely by introducing psychological elements, such as motives and interests, alongside of societal elements. Such additions merely compound the error of the omission. This is the flaw in George Homan's presidential address on "Bringing Man Back In" (*American Sociological Review*, XXIX, No. 6, 809–18).

He has to organize or cut out his lines of conduct on the basis of how he does handle them.

This way of viewing human action is directly opposite to that which dominates psychological and social sciences. In these sciences human action is seen as a product of factors that play upon or through the human actor. Depending on the preference of the scholar, such determining factors may be physiological stimulations, organic drives, needs, feelings, unconscious motives, conscious motives, sentiments, ideas, attitudes, norms, values, role requirements, status demands, cultural prescriptions, institutional pressures or social-system requirements. Regardless of which factors are chosen, either singly or in combination, action is regarded as their product and hence is explained in their terms. The formula is simple: Given factors play on the human being to produce given types of behavior. The formula is frequently amplified so as to read: Under specified conditions, given factors playing on a given organization of the human being will produce a given type of behavior. The formula, in either its simple or amplified form, represents the way in which human action is seen in theory and research. Under the formula the human being becomes a mere medium or forum for the operation of the factors that produce the behavior. Mead's scheme is fundamentally different from this formula. In place of being a mere medium for operation of determining factors that play upon him, the human being is seen as an active organism in his own right, facing, dealing with, and acting toward the objects he indicates. Action is seen as conduct which is constructed by the actor instead of response elicited from some kind of preformed organization in him. We can say that the traditional formula of human action fails to recognize that the human being is a self. Mead's scheme, in contrast, is based on this recognition.

SOCIAL INTERACTION

I can give here only a very brief sketch of Mead's highly illuminating analysis of social interaction. He identified two forms or levels—non-symbolic interaction and symbolic interaction. In non-symbolic interaction human beings respond directly to one another's gestures or actions; in symbolic interaction they interpret each other's gestures and act on the basis of the meaning yielded by the interpretation. An unwitting response to the tone of another's voice illustrates non-symbolic interaction. Interpreting the shaking of a fist as signifying that a person is preparing to attack illustrates symbolic interaction. Mead's concern was predominantly with symbolic interaction. Symbolic interaction involves *interpretation*, or ascertaining the meaning of the actions or remarks of the other person, and *definition*, or conveying indications to another person as to how he is to act. Human association consists of a process of such interpretation and definition. Through this process the participants fit their own acts to the ongoing acts of one another and guide others in doing so.

Several important matters need to be noted in the case of symbolic interaction. First, it is a formative process in its own right. The prevailing practice of psychology and sociology is to treat social interaction as a neutral medium, as a mere forum for the operation of outside factors. Thus psychologists are led to account for the behavior of people in interaction by resorting to elements of the psychological equipment of the participants—such elements as motives, feelings, attitudes, or personality organization. Sociologists do the same sort of thing by resorting to societal factors, such as cultural prescriptions, values, social roles, or structural pressures. Both miss the central point that human interaction is a positive shaping process in its own right. The participants in it have to build up their respective lines of conduct by constant interpretation of each other's ongoing lines of action. As participants take account of each other's ongoing acts, they have to arrest, reorganize, or adjust their own intentions, wishes, feelings, and attitudes; similarly, they have to judge the fitness of norms, values, and group prescriptions for the situation being formed by the acts of others. Factors of psychological equipment and social organization are not substitutes for the interpretative process; they are admissible only in terms of how they are handled in the interpretative process. Symbolic interaction has to be seen and studied in its own right.

Symbolic interaction is noteworthy in a second way. Because of it human group life takes on the character of an ongoing process—a continuing matter of fitting developing lines of conduct to one another. The fitting together of the lines of conduct is done through the dual process of definition and interpretation. This dual process operates both to sustain established patterns of joint conduct and to open them to transformation. Established patterns of group life exist and persist only through the continued use of the same schemes of interpretation; and such schemes of interpretation are maintained only through their continued confirmation by the defining acts of others. It is highly important to recognize that the established patterns of group life just do not carry on by themselves but are dependent for their continuity on recurrent affirmative definition. Let the interpretations that sustain them be undermined or disrupted by changed definitions from others and the patterns can quickly collapse. This dependency of interpretations on the defining acts of others also explains why symbolic interaction conduces so markedly to the transformation of the forms of joint activity that make up group life. In the flow of group life there are innumerable points at which the participants are redefining each other's acts. Such redefinition is very common in adversary relations, it is frequent in group discussion, and it is essentially intrinsic to dealing with problems. (And I may remark here that no human group is free of problems.) Redefinition imparts a formative character to human interaction, giving rise at this or that point to new objects, new conceptions, new relations, and new types of behavior. In short, the reliance on symbolic interaction makes human group life a developing process instead of a mere issue or product of psychological or social structure.

There is a third aspect of symbolic interaction which is important to note. In making the process of interpretation and definition of one another's acts central in human interaction, symbolic interaction is able to cover the full range of the generic forms of human association. It embraces equally well such relationships as cooperation, conflict, domination, exploitation, consensus, disagreement, closely knit identification, and indifferent concern for one another. The participants in each of such relations have the same common task of constructing their acts by interpreting and defining the acts of each other. The significance of this simple observation becomes evident in contrasting symbolic interaction with the various schemes of human interaction that are to be found in the literature. Almost always such schemes construct a general model of human interaction or society on the basis of a particular type of human relationship. An outstanding contemporary instance is Talcott Parsons' scheme which presumes and asserts that the primordial and generic form of human interaction is the "complementarity of expectations." Other schemes depict the basic and generic model of human interaction as being "conflict," others assert it to be "identity through common sentiments," and still other that it is agreement in the form of "consensus." Such schemes are parochial. Their great danger lies in imposing on the breadth of human interaction an image derived from the study of only one form of interaction. Thus, in different hands, human society is said to be fundamentally a sharing of common values; or, conversely, a struggle for power; or, still differently, the exercise of consensus; and so on. The simple point implicit in Mead's analysis of symbolic interaction is that human beings, in interpreting and defining one another's acts, can and do meet each other in the full range of human relations. Proposed schemes of human society should respect this simple point.

OBJECTS

The concept of object is another fundamental pillar in Mead's scheme of analysis. Human beings live in a world or environment of objects, and their activities are formed around objects. This bland statement becomes very significant when it is realized that for Mead objects are human constructs and not self-existing entities with intrinsic natures. Their nature is dependent on the orientation and action of people toward them. Let me spell this out. For Mead, an object is anything that can be designated or referred to. It may be physical as a chair or imaginary as a ghost, natural as a cloud in the sky or man-made as an automobile, material as the Empire State Building or abstract as the concept of liberty, animate as an elephant or inanimate as a vein of coal, inclusive of a class of people as politicians or restricted to a specific person as President de Gaulle, definite as a multiplication table or vague as a philosophical doctrine. In short, objects consist of whatever people indicate or refer to.

There are several important points in this analysis of objects. First, the nature of an object is constituted by the meaning it has for the person or persons for whom it is an object. Second, this meaning is not intrinsic to the object but arises from how the person is

68

initially prepared to act toward it. Readiness to use a chair as something in which to sit gives it the meaning of a chair; to one with no experience with the use of chairs the object would appear with a different meaning, such as a strange weapon. It follows that objects vary in their meaning. A tree is not the same object to a lumberman, a botanist, or a poet; a star is a different object to a modern astronomer than it was to a sheepherder of antiquity; communism is a different object to a Soviet patriot than it is to a Wall Street broker. Third, objects—all objects—are social products in that they are formed and transformed by the defining process that takes place in social interaction. The meaning of the objects—chairs, trees, stars, prostitutes, saints, communism, public education, or whatnot—is formed from the ways in which others refer to such objects or act toward them. Fourth, people are prepared or set to act toward objects on the basis of the meaning of the objects for them. In a genuine sense the organization of a human being consists of his objects, that is, his tendencies to act on the basis of their meanings. Fifth, just because an object is something that is designated, one can organize one's action toward it instead of responding immediately to it; one can inspect the object, think about it, work out a plan of action toward it, or decide whether or not to act toward it. In standing over against the object in both a logical and psychological sense, one is freed from coercive response to it. In this profound sense an object is different from a stimulus as ordinarily conceived.

This analysis of objects puts human group life into a new and interesting perspective. Human beings are seen as living in a world of meaningful objects—not in an environment of stimuli or self-constituted entities. This world is socially produced in that the meanings are fabricated through the process of social interaction. Thus, different groups come to develop different worlds—and these worlds change as the objects that compose them change in meaning. Since people are set to act in terms of the meanings of their objects, the world of objects of a group represents in a genuine sense its action organization. To identify and understand the life of a group it is necessary to identify its world of objects; this identification has to be in terms of the meanings objects have for the members of the group. Finally, people are not locked to their objects; they may check action toward objects and indeed work out new lines of conduct toward them. This condition introduces into human group life an indigenous source of transformation.

JOINT ACTION

I use the term "joint action" in place of Mead's term "social act." It refers to the larger collective form of action that is constituted by the fitting together of the lines of behavior of the separate participants. Illustrations of joint action are a trading transaction, a family dinner, a marriage ceremony, a shopping expedition, a game, a convivial party, a debate, a court trial, or a war. We note in each instance an identifiable and distinctive form of joint action, comprised by an articulation of the acts of the participants. Joint actions range from a simple collaboration of two individuals to a complex alignment of the acts of huge organizations or institutions. Everywhere we look in a human society we see people engaging in forms of joint action. Indeed, the totality of such instances—in all of their multitudinous variety, their variable connections, and their complex networks—constitutes the life of a society. It is easy to understand from these remarks why Mead saw joint action, or the social act, as the distinguishing characteristic of society. For him, the social act was the fundamental unit of society. Its analysis, accordingly, lays bare the generic nature of society.

To begin with, a joint action cannot be resolved into a common or same type of behavior on the part of the participants. Each participant necessarily occupies a different position, acts from that position, and engages in a separate and distinctive act. It is the fitting together of these acts and not their commonality that constitutes joint action. How do these separate acts come to fit together in the case of human society? Their alignment does not occur through sheer mechanical juggling, as in the shaking of walnuts in a jar, or through unwitting adaptation, as in an ecological arrangement in a plant community. Instead, the participants fit their acts together, first, by identifying the social act in which they are about to engage and, second, by interpreting and defining each other's acts in forming the joint act. By identifying the social act or joint action the participant is able to orient himself; he has a key to interpreting the acts of others and a guide for directing his action with regard to them. Thus, to act appropriately, the participant has to identify a marriage ceremony as a marriage ceremony, a holdup as a holdup, a debate as a debate, a war as a war, and so forth. But, even though this identification be made, the participants in the joint action that is being formed still find it necessary to interpret and define one another's ongoing acts. They have to ascertain what the others are doing and plan to do and make indications to one another of what to do.

This brief analysis of joint action enables us to note several matters of distinct importance. It calls attention, first, to the fact that the essence of society lies in an ongoing process of action—not in a posited structure of relations. Without action, any structure of relations between people is meaningless. To be understood, a society must be seen and grasped in terms of the action that comprises it. Next, such action has to be seen and treated, not by tracing the separate lines of action of the participants—whether the participants be single individuals, collectivities, or organizations—but in terms of the joint action into which the separate lines of action fit and merge. Few students of human society have fully grasped this point or its implications. Third, just because it is built up over time by the fitting together of acts, each joint action must be seen as having a career or a history. In having a career, its course and fate are contingent on what happens during its formation. Fourth, this career is generally orderly, fixed and repetitious by virtue of a common identification or definition of the joint action that is made by its participants. The common definition supplies each participant with decisive guidance in directing his own act so as to fit into the acts of the others. Such common definitions serve, above everything else, to account for the regularity, stability, and repetitiveness of joint action in vast areas of group life; they are the source of the established and regulated social behavior that is envisioned in the concept of culture. Fifth, however, the career of joint actions also must be seen as open to many possibilities of uncertainty. Let me specify the more important of these possibilities. One, joint actions have to be initiated—and they may not be. Two, once started a joint action may be interrupted, abandoned, or transformed. Three, the participants may not make a common definition of the joint action into which they are thrown and hence may orient their acts on different premises. Four, a common definition of a joint action may still allow

71

wide differences in the direction of the separate lines of action and hence in the course taken by the joint action; a war is a good example. Five, new situations may arise calling for hitherto unexisting types of joint action, leading to confused exploratory efforts to work out a fitting together of acts. And, six, even in the context of a commonly defined joint action, participants may be led to rely on other considerations in interpreting and defining each other's lines of action. Time does not allow me to spell out and illustrate the importance of these possibilities. To mention them should be sufficient, however, to show that uncertainty, contingency, and transformation are part and parcel of the process of joint action. To assume that the diversified joint actions which comprise a human society are set to follow fixed and established channels is a sheer gratuitous assumption.

From the foregoing discussion of the self, the act, social interaction, objects, and joint action we can sketch a picture of human society. The picture is composed in terms of action. A society is seen as people meeting the varieties of situations that are thrust on them by their conditions of life. These situations are met by working out joint actions in which participants have to align their acts to one another. Each participant does so by interpreting the acts of others and, in turn, by making indications to others as to how they should act. By virtue of this process of interpretation and definition joint actions are built up; they have careers. Usually, the course of a joint action is outlined in advance by the fact that the participants make a common identification of it; this makes for regularity, stability, and repetitiveness in the joint action. However, there are many joint actions that encounter obstructions, that have no pre-established pathways, and that have to be constructed along new lines. Mead saw human society in this way—as a diversified social process in which people were engaged in forming joint actions to deal with situations confronting them.

This picture of society stands in significant contrast to the dominant views of society in the social and psychological sciences—even to those that pretend to view society as action. To point out the major differences in the contrast is the best way of specifying the sociological implications of Mead's scheme of thought.

The chief difference is that the dominant views in sociology and psychology fail, alike, to see human beings as organisms having selves. Instead, they regard human beings as merely responding organisms and, accordingly, treat action as mere response to factors playing on human beings. This is exemplified in the efforts to account for human behavior by such factors as motives, ego demands, attitudes, role requirements, values, status expectations, and structural stresses. In such approaches the human being becomes a mere medium through which such initiating factors operate to produce given actions. From Mead's point of view such a conception grossly misrepresents the nature of human beings and human action. Mead's scheme interposes a process of self-interaction between initiating factors and the action that may follow in their wake. By virtue of self-interaction the human being becomes an acting organism coping with situations in place of being an organism merely responding to the play of factors. And his action becomes something he constructs and directs to meet the situations in place of an unrolling of reactions evoked from him. In introducing the self, Mead's position focuses on how human beings handle and fashion their world, not on disparate responses to imputed factors.

If human beings are, indeed, organisms with selves, and if their action is, indeed, an outcome of a process of self-interaction, schemes that purport to study and explain social action should respect and accommodate these features. To do so, current schemes in sociology and psychology would have to undergo radical revision. They would have to shift from a preoccupation with initiating factor and terminal result to a preoccupation with a process of formation. They would have to view action as something constructed by the actor instead of something evoked from him. They would have to depict the milieu of action in terms of how the milieu appears to the actor in place of how it appears to the outside student. They would have to incorporate the interpretive process which at present they scarcely deign to touch. They would have to recognize that any given act has a career in which it is constructed but in which it may be interrupted, held in abeyance, abandoned, or recast.

On the methodological or research side the study of action would have to be made from the position of the actor. Since action is forged by the actor out of what he perceives, interprets, and judges, one would have to see the operating situation as the actor sees it, perceive objects as the actor perceives them, ascertain their meaning in terms of the meaning they have for the actor, and follow the actor's line of conduct as the actor organizes it—in short, one would have to take the role of the actor and see his world from his standpoint. This methodological approach stands in contrast to the so-called objective approach so dominant today, namely, that of viewing the actor and his action from the perspective of an outside, detached observer. The "objective" approach holds the danger of the observer substituting his view of the field of action for the view held by the actor. It is unnecessary to add that the actor acts toward his world on the basis of how he sees it and not on the basis of how that world appears to the outside observer.

In continuing the discussion of this matter, I wish to consider especially what we might term the structural conception of human society. This conception views society as established organization, familiar to us in the use of such terms as social structure, social system, status position, social role, social stratification, institutional structure, cultural pattern, social codes, social norms, and social values. The conception presumes that a human society is structured with regard to (a) the social positions occupied by the people in it and with regard to (b) the patterns of behavior in which they engage. It is presumed further that this interlinked structure of social positions and behavior patterns is the over-all determinant of social action; this is evidenced, of course, in the practice of explaining conduct by such structural concepts as role requirements, status demands, strata differences, cultural prescriptions, values, and norms. Social action falls into two general categories: conformity, marked by adherence to the structure, and deviance, marked by departure from it. Because of the central and determinative position into which it is elevated, structure becomes necessarily the encompassing object of sociological study and analysis—epitomized by the well-nigh universal assertion that a human group or society is a "social system." It is perhaps unnecessary to observe that the conception of human society as structure or organization is ingrained in the very marrow of contemporary sociology.

Mead's scheme definitely challenges this conception. It sees human society not as an established structure but as people meeting their conditions of life; it sees social action not as an emanation of societal structure but as a formation made by human actors; it sees this formation of action not as societal factors coming to expression through the medium of human organisms but as constructions made by actors out of what they take into account; it sees group life not as a release or expression of established structure but as a process of building up joint actions; it sees social actions as having variable careers and not as confined to the alternatives of conformity to or deviation from the dictates of established structure; it sees the so-called interaction between parts of a society not as a direct exercising of influence by one part on another but as mediated throughout by interpretations made by people; accordingly, it sees society not as a system, whether in the form of a static, moving, or whatever kind of equilibrium, but as a vast number of occurring joint actions, many closely linked, many not linked at all, many prefigured and repetitious, others being carved out in new directions, and all being pursued to serve the purposes of the participants and not the requirements of a system. I have said enough, I think, to point out the drastic differences between the Meadian conception of society and the widespread sociological conceptions of it as a structure.

The differences do not mean, incidentally, that Mead's view rejects the existence of structure in human society. Such a position would be ridiculous. There are such matters as social roles, status positions, rank orders, bureaucratic organizations, relations between institutions, differential authority arrangements, social codes, norms, values, and the like. And they are very important. But their importance does not lie in an alleged determination of action nor in an alleged existence as parts of a self-operating societal system. Instead, they are important only as they enter into the process of interpretation and definition out of which joint actions are formed. The manner and extent to which they enter may vary greatly from situation to situation, depending on what people take into account and how they assess what they take account of. Let me give one brief illustration. It is ridiculous, for instance, to assert, as a number of eminent sociologists have done, that social interaction is an interaction between social roles. Social interaction is obviously an interaction between *people* and not between roles; the needs of the participants are to interpret and handle what confronts them—such as a topic of conversation or a problem—and not to give expression to their roles. It is only in highly ritualistic relations that the direction and content of conduct can be explained by roles. Usually, the direction and content are fashioned out of what people in interaction have to deal with. That roles affect in varying degree phases of the direction and content of action is true but is a matter of determination in given cases. This is a far cry from asserting action to be a product of roles. The observation I have made in this brief discussion of social roles applies with equal validity to all other structural matters.

Another significant implication of Mead's scheme of thought refers to the question of what holds a human society together. As we know, this question is converted by sociologists into a problem of unity, stability, and orderliness. And, as we know further, the typical answer given by sociologists is that unity, stability, and orderliness come from a sharing in common of certain basic matters, such as codes, sentiments, and, above all, values. Thus, the disposition is to regard common values as the glue that holds a society together, as the controlling regulator that brings and keeps the activities in a society in orderly relationship, and as the force that preserves stability in a society. Conversely, it is held that conflict between values or the disintegration of values creates disunity, disorder, and instability. This conception of human society becomes subject to great modification if we think of society as consisting of the fitting together of acts to form joint action. Such alignment may take place for any number of reasons, depending on the situations calling for joint action, and need not involve, or spring from, the sharing of common values. The participants may fit their acts to one another in orderly joint actions on the basis of compromise, out of duress, because they may use one another in achieving their respective ends, because it is the sensible thing to do, or out of sheer necessity. This is particularly likely to be true in our modern complex societies with their great diversity in composition, in lines of interest, and in their respective worlds of concern. In very large measure, society becomes the formation of workable relations. To seek to encompass, analyze, and understand the life of a society on the assumption that the existence of a society necessarily depends on the sharing of values can lead to strained treatment, gross misrepresentation, and faulty lines of interpretation. I believe that the Meadian perspective, in posing the question of how people are led to align their acts in different situations in place of presuming that this necessarily requires and stems from a sharing of common values, is a more salutary and realistic approach.

There are many other significant sociological implications in Mead's scheme of thought which, under the limit of space, I can do no more than mention. Socialization shifts its character from being an effective internalization of norms and values to a cultivated capacity to take the roles of others effectively. Social control becomes fundamentally and necessarily a matter of self-control. Social change becomes a continuous indigenous process in human group life instead of an episodic result of extraneous facts playing on established structure. Human group life is seen as always incomplete and undergoing development instead of jumping from one completed state to another. Social disorganization is seen not as a breakdown of existing structure but as an inability to mobilize action effectively in the face of a given situation. Social action, since it has a career, is recognized as having a historical dimension which has to be taken into account in order to be adequately understood.

In closing I wish to say that my presentation has necessarily skipped much in Mead's scheme that is of great significance. Further, I have not sought to demonstrate the validity of his analyses. However, I have tried to suggest the freshness, the fecundity, and the revolutionary implications of his point of view.

Society as Symbolic Interaction

A view of human society as symbolic interaction has been followed more than it has been formulated. Partial, usually fragmentary, statements of it are to be found in the writings of a number of eminent scholars, some inside the field of sociology and some outside. Among the former we may note such scholars as Charles Horton Cooley, W. I. Thomas, Robert E. Parks, E. W. Burgess, Florian Znaniecki, Ellsworth Faris, and James Mickel Williams. Among those outside the discipline we may note William James, John Dewey, and George Herbert Mead. None of these scholars, in my judgment, has presented a systematic statement of the nature of human group life from the standpoint of symbolic interaction. Mead stands out among all of them in laying bare the fundamental premises of the approach, yet he did little to develop its methodological implications for sociological study. Students who seek to depict the position of symbolic interaction may easily give different pictures of it. What I have to present should be regarded as my personal version. My aim is to present the basic premises of the point of view and to develop their methodological consequences for the study of human group life.

The term "symbolic interaction" refers, of course, to the peculiar

"Society as Symbolic Interaction," Arnold Rose, ed., **Human Behavior and Social Processes,** *reprinted by permission of Houghton Mifflin Co.*

and distinctive character of interaction as it takes place between human beings. The peculiarity consists in the fact that human beings interpret or "define" each other's actions instead of merely reacting to each other's actions. Their "response" is not made directly to the actions of one another but instead is based on the meaning which they attach to such actions. Thus, human interaction is mediated by the use of symbols, by interpretation, or by ascertaining the meaning of one another's actions. This mediation is equivalent to inserting a process of interpretation between stimulus and response in the case of human behavior.

The simple recognition that human beings interpret each other's actions as the means of acting toward one another has permeated the thought and writings of many scholars of human conduct and of human group life. Yet few of them have endeavored to analyze what such interpretation implies about the nature of the human being or about the nature of human association. They are usually content with a mere recognition that "interpretation" should be caught by the student, or with a simple realization that symbols, such as cultural norms or values, must be introduced into their analyses. Only G. H. Mead, in my judgment, has sought to think through what the act of interpretation implies for an understanding of the human being, human action, and human association. The essentials of his analysis are so penetrating and profound and so important for an understanding of human group life that I wish to spell them out, even though briefly.

The key feature in Mead's analysis is that the human being has a self. This idea should not be cast aside as esoteric or glossed over as something that is obvious and hence not worthy of attention. In declaring that the human being has a self, Mead had in mind chiefly that the human being can be the object of his own actions. He can act toward himself as he might act toward others. Each of us is familiar with actions of this sort in which the human being gets angry with himself, rebuffs himself, takes pride in himself, argues with himself, tries to bolster his own courage, tells himself that he should "do this" or not "do that," sets goals for himself, makes compromises with himself, and plans what he is going to do. That the human being acts toward himself in these and countless other ways is a matter of easy empirical observation. To recognize that the human being can act toward himself is no mystical conjuration.

Mead regards this ability of the human being to act toward himself as the central mechanism with which the human being faces and deals with his world. This mechanism enables the human being to make indications to himself of things in his surroundings and thus to guide his actions by what he notes. Anything of which a human being is conscious is something which he is indicating to himself—the ticking of a clock, a knock at the door, the appearance of a friend, the remark made by a companion, a recognition that he has a task to perform, or the realization that he has a cold. Conversely, anything of which he is not conscious is, *ipso facto*, something which he is not indicating to himself. The conscious life of the human being, from the time that he awakens until he falls asleep, is a continual flow of self-indications—notations of the things with which he deals and takes into account. We are given, then, a picture of the human being as an organism which confronts its world with a mechanism for making indications to itself. This is the mechanism that is involved in interpreting the actions of others. To interpret the actions of another is to point out to oneself that the action has this or that meaning or character.

Now, according to Mead, the significance of making indications to oneself is of paramount importance. The importance lies along two lines. First, to indicate something is to extricate it from its setting, to hold it apart, to give it a meaning or, in Mead's language, to make it into an object. An object—that is to say, anything that an individual indicates to himself—is different from a stimulus; instead of having an intrinsic character which acts on the individual and which can be identified apart from the individual, its character or meaning is conferred on it by the individual. The object is a product of the individual's disposition to act instead of being an antecedent stimulus which evokes the act. Instead of the individual being surrounded by an environment of pre-existing objects which play upon him and call forth his behavior, the proper picture is that he constructs his objects on the basis of his on-going activity. In any of his countless acts—whether minor, like dressing himself, or major, like organizing himself for a professional career—the individual is designating different objects to himself, giving them meaning, judging their suitability to his action, and making decisions on the basis of the judgment. This is what is meant by interpretation or acting on the basis of symbols.

80

The second important implication of the fact that the human being makes indications to himself is that his action is constructed or built up instead of being a mere release. Whatever the action in which he is engaged, the human individual proceeds by pointing out to himself the divergent things which have to be taken into account in the course of his action. He has to note what he wants to do and how he is to do it; he has to point out to himself the various conditions which may be instrumental to his action and those which may obstruct his action; he has to take account of the demands, the expectations, the prohibitions, and the threats as they may arise in the situation in which he is acting. His action is built up step by step through a process of such self-indication. The human individual pieces together and guides his action by taking account of different things and interpreting their significance for his prospective action. There is no instance of conscious action of which this is not true.

The process of constructing action through making indications to oneself cannot be swallowed up in any of the conventional psychological categories. This process is distinct from and different from what is spoken of as the "ego"—just as it is different from any other conception which conceives of the self in terms of composition or organization. Self-indication is a moving communicative process in which the individual notes things, assesses them, gives them a meaning, and decides to act on the basis of the meaning. The human being stands over against the world, or against "alters," with such a process and not with a mere ego. Further, the process of self-indication cannot be subsumed under the forces, whether from the outside or inside, which are presumed to play upon the individual to produce his behavior. Environmental pressures, external stimuli, organic drives, wishes, attitudes, feelings, ideas, and their like do not cover or explain the process of self-indication. The process of self-indication stands over against them in that the individual points out to himself and interprets the appearance or expression of such things, noting a given social demand that is made on him, recognizing a command, observing that he is hungry, realizing that he wishes to buy something, aware that he has a given feeling, conscious that he dislikes eating with someone he despises, or aware that he is thinking of doing some given thing. By virtue of indicating such things to himself, he places himself over against them and is able to act back against them, accepting them, rejecting them, or transforming them in accordance with how he defines or interprets them. His behavior, accordingly, is not a result of such things as environmental pressures, stimuli, motives, attitudes, and ideas but arises instead from how he interprets and handles these things in the action which he is constructing. The process of self-indication by means of which human action is formed cannot be accounted for by factors which precede the act. The process of self-indication exists in its own right and must be accepted and studied as such. It is through this process that the human being constructs his conscious action.

Now Mead recognizes that the formation of action by the individual through a process of self-indication always takes place in a social context. Since this matter is so vital to an understanding of symbolic interaction it needs to be explained carefully. Fundamentally, group action takes the form of a fitting together of individual lines of action. Each individual aligns his action to the action of others by ascertaining what they are doing or what they intend to do—that is, by getting the meaning of their acts. For Mead, this is done by the individual "taking the role" of others—either the role of a specific person or the role of a group (Mead's "generalized other"). In taking such roles the individual seeks to ascertain the intention or direction of the acts of others. He forms and aligns his own action on the basis of such interpretation of the acts of others. This is the fundamental way in which group action takes place in human society.

The foregoing are the essential features, as I see them, in Mead's analysis of the bases of symbolic interaction. They presuppose the following: that human society is made up of individuals who have selves (that is, make indications to themselves); that individual action is a construction and not a release, being built up by the individual through noting and interpreting features of the situations in which he acts; that group or collective action consists of the aligning of individual actions, brought about by the individuals' interpreting or taking into account each other's actions. Since my purpose is to present and not to defend the position of symbolic interaction I shall not endeavor in this essay to advance support for the three premises which I have just indicated. I wish merely to say that the three premises can be easily verified empirically. I know of no instance of human group action to which the three permises do not apply. The reader is challenged to find or think of a single instance which they do not fit.

I wish now to point out that sociological views of human society are, in general, markedly at variance with the premises which I have indicated as underlying symbolic interaction. Indeed, the predominant number of such views, especially those in vogue at the present time, do not see or treat human society as symbolic interaction. Wedded, as they tend to be, to some form of sociological determinism, they adopt images of human society, of individuals in it, and of group action which do not square with the premises of symbolic interaction. I wish to say a few words about the major lines of variance.

Sociological thought rarely recognizes or treats human societies as composed of individuals who have selves. Instead, they assume human beings to be merely organisms with some kind of organization, responding to forces which play upon them. Generally, although not exclusively, these forces are lodged in the make-up of the society, as in the case of "social system," "social structure," "culture," "status position," "social role," "custom," "institution," "collective representation," "social situation," "social norm," and "values." The assumption is that the behavior of people as members of *a society* is an expression of the play on them of these kinds of factors or forces. This, of course, is the logical position which is necessarily taken when the scholar explains their behavior or phases of their behavior in terms of one or another of such social factors. The individuals who compose a human society are treated as the media through which such factors operate, and the social action of such individuals is regarded as an expression of such factors. This approach or point of view denies, or at least ignores, that human beings have selves— that they act by making indications to themselves. Incidentally, the "self" is not brought into the picture by introducing such items as organic drives, motives, attitudes, feelings, internalized social factors, or psychological components. Such psychological factors have the same status as the social factors mentioned: they are regarded as factors which play on the individual to produce his action. They do not constitute the process of self-indication. The process of self-indication stands over against them, just as it stands over against the social factors which play on the human being. Practically all sociological conceptions of human society fail to recognize that the individuals who compose it have selves in the sense spoken of.

Correspondingly, such sociological conceptions do not regard the

83

social actions of individuals in human society as being constructed by them through a process of interpretation. Instead, action is treated as a product of factors which play on and through individuals. The social behavior of people is not seen as built up by them through an interpretation of objects, situations, or the actions of others. If a place is given to "interpretation," the interpretation is regarded as merely an expression of other factors (such as motives) which precede the act, and accordingly disappears as a factor in its own right. Hence, the social action of people is treated as an outward flow or expression of forces playing on them rather than as acts which are built up by people through their interpretation of the situations in which they are placed.

These remarks suggest another significant line of difference between general sociological views and the position of symbolic interaction. These two sets of views differ in where they lodge social action. Under the perspective of symbolic interaction, social action is lodged in acting individuals who fit their respective lines of action to one another through a process of interpretation; group action is the collective action of such individuals. As opposed to this view, sociological conceptions generally lodge social action in the action of society or in some unit of society. Examples of this are legion. Let me cite a few. Some conceptions, in treating societies or human groups as "social systems," regard group action as an expression of a system, either in a state of balance or seeking to achieve balance. Or group action is conceived as an expression of the "functions" of a society or of a group. Or group action is regarded as the outward expression of elements lodged in society or the group, such as cultural demands, societal purposes, social values, or institutional stresses. These typical conceptions ignore or blot out a view of group life or of group action as consisting of the collective or concerted actions of individuals seeking to meet their life situations. If recognized at all, the efforts of people to develop collective acts to meet their situations are subsumed under the play of underlying or transcending forces which are lodged in society or its parts. The individuals composing the society or the group become "carriers," or media for the expression of such forces; and the interpretative behavior by means of which people form their actions is merely a coerced link in the play of such forces.

The indication of the foregoing lines of variance should help to put the position of symbolic interaction in better perspective. In the remaining discussion I wish to sketch somewhat more fully how human society appears in terms of symbolic interaction and to point out some methodological implications.

Human society is to be seen as consisting of acting people, and the life of the society is to be seen as consisting of their actions. The acting units may be separate individuals, collectivities whose members are acting together on a common quest, or organizations acting on behalf of a constituency. Respective examples are individual purchasers in a market, a play group or missionary band, and a business corporation or a national professional association. There is no empirically observable activity in a human society that does not spring from some acting unit. This banal statement needs to be stressed in light of the common practice of sociologists of reducing human society to social units that do not act—for example, social classes in modern society. Obviously, there are ways of viewing human society other than in terms of the acting units that compose it. I merely wish to point out that in respect to concrete or empirical activity human society must necessarily be seen in terms of the acting units that form it. I would add that any scheme of human society claiming to be a realistic analysis has to respect and be congruent with the empirical recognition that a human society consists of acting units.

Corresponding respect must be shown to the conditions under which such units act. One primary condition is that action takes place in and with regard to a situation. Whatever be the acting unit —an individual, a family, a school, a church, a business firm, a labor union, a legislature, and so on—any particular action is formed in the light of the situation in which it takes place. This leads to the recognition of a second major condition, namely, that the action is formed or constructed by interpreting the situation. The acting unit necessarily has to identify the things which it has to take into account— tasks, opportunities, obstacles, means, demands, discomforts, dangers, and the like; it has to assess them in some fashion and it has to make decisions on the basis of the assessment. Such interpretative behavior may take place in the individual guiding his own action, in a collectivity of individuals acting in concert, or in "agents" acting on behalf of a group or organization. Group life consists of acting units developing acts to meet the situations in which they are placed.

Usually, most of the situations encountered by people in a given society are defined or "structured" by them in the same way. Through previous interaction they develop and acquire common understandings or definitions of how to act in this or that situation. These common definitions enable people to act alike. The common repetitive behavior of people in such situations should not mislead the student into believing that no process of interpretation is in play; on the contrary, even though fixed, the actions of the participating people are constructed by them through a process of interpretation. Since ready-made and commonly accepted definitions are at hand, little strain is placed on people in guiding and organizing their acts. However, many other situations may not be defined in a single way by the participating people. In this event, their lines of action do not fit together readily and collective action is blocked. Interpretations have to be developed and effective accommodation of the participants to one another has to be worked out. In the case of such "undefined" situations, it is necessary to trace and study the emerging process of definition which is brought into play.

Insofar as sociologists or students of human society are concerned with the behavior of acting units, the position of symbolic interaction requires the student to catch the process of interpretation through which they construct their actions. This process is not to be caught merely by turning to conditions which are antecedent to the process. Such antecedent conditions are helpful in understanding the process insofar as they enter into it, but as mentioned previously they do not constitute the process. Nor can one catch the process merely by inferring its nature from the overt action which is its product. To catch the process, the student must take the role of the acting unit whose behavior he is studying. Since the interpretation is being made by the acting unit in terms of objects designated and appraised, meanings acquired, and decisions made, the process has to be seen from the standpoint of the acting unit. It is the recognition of this fact that makes the research work of such scholars as R. E. Park and W. I. Thomas so notable. To try to catch the interpretative process by remaining aloof as a so-called "objective" observer and refusing to take the role of the acting unit is to risk the worst kind of subjectivism—the objective observer is likely to fill in the process of interpretation with his own surmises in place of catching the process as it occurs in the experience of the acting unit which uses it.

By and large, of course, sociologists do not study human society in terms of its acting units. Instead, they are disposed to view human society in terms of structure or organization and to treat social action as an expression of such structure or organization. Thus, reliance is placed on such structural categories as social system, culture, norms, values, social stratification, status positions, social roles and institutional organization. These are used both to analyze human society and to account for social action within it. Other major interests of sociological scholars center around this focal theme of organization. One line of interest is to view organization in terms of the functions it is supposed to perform. Another line of interest is to study societal organization as a system seeking equilibrium; here the scholar endeavors to detect mechanisms which are indigenous to the system. Another line of interest is to identify forces which play upon organization to bring about changes in it; here the scholar endeavors, especially through comparative study, to isolate a relation between causative factors and structural results. These various lines of sociological perspective and interest, which are so strongly entrenched today, leap over the acting units of a society and bypass the interpretative process by which such acting units build up their actions.

These respective concerns with organization on one hand and with acting units on the other hand set the essential difference between conventional views of human society and the view of it implied in symbolic interaction. The latter view recognizes the presence of organization to human society and respects its importance. However, it sees and treats organization differently. The difference is along two major lines. First, from the standpoint of symbolic interaction the organization of a human society is the framework inside of which social action takes place and is not the determinant of that action. Second, such organization and changes in it are the product of the activity of acting units and not of "forces" which leave such acting units out of account. Each of these two major lines of difference should be explained briefly in order to obtain a better understanding of how human society appears in terms of symbolic interaction.

From the standpoint of symbolic interaction, social organization is a framework inside of which acting units develop their actions. Structural features, such as "culture," "social systems," "social stratification," or "social roles," set conditions for their action but do not determine their action. People—that is, acting units—do not act toward culture, social structure or the like; they act toward situations. Social organization enters into action only to the extent to which it shapes situations in which people act, and to the extent to which it supplies fixed sets of symbols which people use in interpreting their situations. These two forms of influence of social organization are important. In the case of settled and stabilized societies, such as isolated primitive tribes and peasant communities, the influence is certain to be profound. In the case of human societies, particularly modern societies, in which streams of new situations arise and old situations become unstable, the influence of organization decreases. One should bear in mind that the most important element confronting an acting unit in situations is the actions of other acting units. In modern society, with its increasing criss-crossing of lines of action, it is common for situations to arise in which the actions of participants are not previously regularized and standardized. To this extent, existing social organization does not shape the situations. Correspondingly, the symbols or tools of interpretation used by acting units in such situations may vary and shift considerably. For these reasons, social action may go beyond, or depart from, existing organization in any of its structural dimensions. The organization of a human society is not to be identified with the process of interpretation used by its acting units; even though it affects that process, it does not embrace or cover the process.

Perhaps the most outstanding consequence of viewing human society as organization is to overlook the part played by acting units in social change. The conventional procedure of sociologists is (a) to identify human society (or some part of it) in terms of an established or organized form, (b) to identify some factor or condition of change playing upon the human society or the given part of it, and (c) to identify the new form assumed by the society following upon the play of the factor of change. Such observations permit the student to couch propositions to the effect that a given factor of change playing upon a given organized form results in a given new organized form. Examples ranging from crude to refined statements are legion, such as that an economic depression increases solidarity in the families of workingmen or that industrialization replaces extended families by nuclear families. My concern here is not with the validity of such propositions but with the methodological position which they presuppose. Essentially, such propositions either ignore the role of the interpretative behavior of acting units in the given instance of change, or else regard the interpretative behavior as coerced by the factor of change. I wish to point out that any line of social change, since it involves change in human action, is necessarily mediated by interpretation on the part of the people caught up in the change—the change appears in the form of new situations in which people have to construct new forms of action. Also, in line with what has been said previously, interpretations of new situations are not predetermined by conditions antecedent to the situations but depend on what is taken into account and assessed in the actual situations in which behavior is formed. Variations in interpretation may readily occur as different acting units cut out different objects in the situation, or give different weight to the objects which they note, or piece objects together in different patterns. In formulating propositions of social change, it would be wise to recognize that any given line of such change is mediated by acting units interpreting the situations with which they are confronted.

Students of human society will have to face the question of whether their preoccupation with categories of structure and organization can be squared with the interpretative process by means of which human beings, individually and collectively, act in human society. It is the discrepancy between the two which plagues such students in their efforts to attain scientific propositions of the sort achieved in the physical and biological sciences. It is this discrepancy, further, which is chiefly responsible for their difficulty in fitting hypothetical propositions to new arrays of empirical data. Efforts are made, of course, to overcome these shortcomings by devising new structural categories, by formulating new structural hypotheses, by developing more refined techniques of research, and even by formulating new methodological schemes of a structural character. These efforts continue to ignore or to explain away the interpretative process by which people act, individually and collectively, in society. The question remains whether human society or social action can be successfully analyzed by schemes which refuse to recognize human beings as they are, namely, as persons constructing individual and collective action through an interpretation of the situations which confront them.

4

Attitudes and the Social Act[*]

This paper is a critical assessment of the concept of attitude as a tool for the study and analysis of human conduct. The vast commitment to the concept of attitude in contemporary theory and research rests obviously on two beliefs. One belief is that the concept is unquestionably suited to analyze and explain human conduct. The other belief is that the concept qualifies as a scientific concept and thus that through appropriate research a body of scientific knowledge can be developed.

In my judgment careful analysis shows that both of these beliefs are false. The concept of attitude as it is currently held rests on a fallacious picture of human action. Also, it fails miserably to meet the requirements of a scientific concept. The task of my paper is to sustain these two serious charges. I wish to consider them in reverse order.

[*] Address as President of the Society for the Study of Social Problems at the annual meeting held jointly with the American Sociological Society and the Rural Sociological Society in Washington, D.C., August 30–September 2, 1955.

Reprinted from Social Problems, Vol. 3, No. 2 (October 1955), 59–65, by permission of The Society for the Study of Social Problems.

ATTITUDE AS A SCIENTIFIC CONCEPT

A satisfactory concept in empirical science must meet three simple requirements: 1. it must point clearly to the individual instances of the class of empirical objects to which it refers; 2. it must distinguish clearly this class of objects from other related classes of objects; and 3. it must enable the development of cumulative knowledge of the class of objects to which it refers. These requirements are, of course, interlocked. A clear identification of the individual instances of the class of objects enables one to study them carefully and through such study to develop a body of knowledge about the class. One may use individual instances to check assertions or hypotheses made about the nature of the class. Further, the ability to identify the individual instances of the class enables one to set the class apart from other classes and thus to relate their covering concepts to one another. This linking of concepts is essential to effective theorizing.

The concept of attitude as currently held fails to meet any of these three simple requirements: it has no clear and fixed empirical reference, its class of objects cannot be distinguished effectively from related classes of objects, and it does not enable the enlargement of knowledge of the class of objects to which it presumably refers. Let me make this clear.

The concept of attitude is empirically ambiguous. We do not have any set of reliable marks or characteristics which enable us properly to identify attitudes in the empirical world we study. An attitude is not perceived directly but must be pieced together through a process of inference. We need to know what to piece together. The current concept of attitude just does not tell what to piece together. We are at a loss to know what data to include as part of an attitude and what to reject as not belonging to an attitude. Not knowing what enters into an attitude, we obviously lack guidance in selecting the kinds of data needed to identify or to delimit the attitude. Instead, we have to proceed arbitrarily, either relying on our personal impressions of what to include or else falling back on some technical device, such as a measurement scale. The technical device, of course, is based on a preconception of what enters into an attitude, tailored in addition to meet certain standards of quantification. It does not address the question of what enters empirically into attitudes as a class.

The consequence of this empirical ambiguity of the concept of attitude is that the concept becomes a mere logical or omnibus term. It covers an unbelievably wide array of concrete instances but is devoid of any generic features which have been isolated through empirical study. It does not refer to a distinguishable class of objects. This condition is sharply reflected in the indeterminate relation between the concept of attitude and other concepts in its order of concern. We cannot effectively distinguish it from, or relate it to, such other concepts as impulses, drives, appetites, antipathies, feelings, sentiments, habits, ideas, opinions, judgments, and decisions. Some twenty years ago Gordon Allport made a valiant but futile effort to show how attitudes differ from such psychological items as those mentioned. I know of no successful effort to do this. Actually, people in the field of attitude study are strangely indifferent to the problem. Here we are, seriously entertaining the concept of attitude as a tool for analyzing human conduct and human makeup; yet we cannot bring it effectively inside an order of established analytical concepts engaged in the same task. Lacking any decisive empirical reference, it blocks solid theorizing. We cannot use it effectively in our theories either as a unit of personal organization or as an element of human action.

An even more serious consequence of not pinning down the concept of attitude empirically has been the inability to develop any cumulative body of knowledge of what an attitude is. Despite the vast number of studies of attitudes that have been made over the years, I am unable to find that they have contributed one iota to knowledge of the generic nature of attitudes. We know no more today about the nature of attitudes than we did thirty-five years ago. We must rule out alleged contributions such as that attitudes are socially formed or that they can be changed. Such assertions tell us nothing about what an attitude is and, as propositions, could have been made with as much value and validity without any concept of attitude. Similarly, interesting procedural findings with regard to precautions in interviewing, wording of questions, and construction of scales have not yielded any generic knowledge of attitudes.

One may appropriately ask, I think, what are we doing if we are engaged in a vast amount of study and research, commanding many of our best minds, only to discover that all of this vast work yields no knowledge of the class of objects we are presumably studying. This does not seem to be the way of science.

The foregoing remarks explain why I think the concept of attitude in its present form is seriously deficient as a scientific concept. The ambiguity of its empirical character prevents the concept of attitude from entering into fruitful and self-correcting relations with the empirical world, blocks its incorporation into a body of analytical theory, and impedes the development of knowledge about its nature.

This, however, is the less important of the two points which I wish to consider. Of greater importance is the fact that it presupposes a fallacious picture of human action.

ATTITUDE AS AN EXPLANATION OF HUMAN ACTION

The use of the concept of attitude to explain behavior rests on a simple logic. The attitude is conceived to be a tendency, a state of preparation, or a state of readiness, which lies behind action, directs action, and moulds action. Thus, the attitude or tendency to act is used to explain and account for the given type of action. Further, the knowledge of the attitude enables one to forecast the kind of action which would take place if the attitude were activated. Actually, the contention that the attitude directs and controls the act is a wholesale begging of the question. The available evidence provides no proof for the contention. There are two conceivable lines of proof. One would be to show through an adequate array of cases a close conformity of action to the previously asserted attitudes, the other would be to trace out meticulously the actual play of the attitude into the act.

Attitude studies do not provide the first line of proof. The overwhelming proportion of attitude studies do not even attempt to concern themselves with action subsequent to the study; accordingly, they tell us nothing of the relation of attitude to action. In the smaller number of instances where some effort has been made to establish a relation the evidence is unconvincing. Sometimes a reasonably high correlation has been found, usually between scores on attitude tests and some index of overt behavior. In other instances, frequently on the same test, the correlation has been low. One will find in the literature well chosen examples where prediction worked out well. Such examples do not represent the known universe of attitude studies or even the universe of the better studies and, hence, do not constitute proof. The matter is made worse by the ability to select impressive cases where prediction failed. Any fair appraisal of the known universe of attitude studies forces one to conclude that no high conformity has been established between asserted attitudes and subsequent action. I realize, of course, that workers in this field believe that deficiencies in prediction will be overcome with the improvement of instruments of attitude study. I merely point out that this view continues to beg the question of whether the attitude controls the act.

The other line of proof would be to demonstrate through an analytical breakdown of the act that a tendency to act does indeed direct and shape the act. Instead of merely correlating the two ends of the act—the tendency and the overt behavior—one would trace out in a step-by-step manner how the tendency played into the developing act, shaped wishes and impulses, fashioned perception, determined selections and dictated decisions. Such meticulous proof would be most convincing. It is almost unnecessary to say that such proof does not exist.

I do not wish to let the matter rest with this type of conclusion. Instead, I wish to undertake an analysis of the human social act to show the falsity of the premise that the tendency or attitude directs and determines the act. In doing so, I shall follow the line of thought of George H. Mead, who above all students has probed deepest into the character of the human act.

The idea that the tendency to act determines that act presupposes that action is no more than a release of what is already organized. The tendency when activated is held to go over directly into activity, which it guides and shapes. Against this picture I submit that a realistic analysis of the human act reveals an entirely different picture. The human act is not a release of an already organized tendency; it is a construction built up by the actor. Instead of a direct translation of the tendency into the act there is an intervening process which is responsible for the form and direction taken by the developing act. As Mead has shown—incidentally, his major contribution to social psychology—this intervening process is constituted by a flow of self interaction in which the individual indicates various things and objects to himself, defines them, judges them, selects from among them, pieces together his selections, and thereby organizes himself to act. It would be a grievous error to assume that this intervening process through which the human actor constructs his act is nothing but the tendency working itself out. Quite the contrary, this intervening process works back on the tendency, sometimes guiding it, sometimes shaping it, sometimes transforming it, sometimes blocking it, and sometimes ruthlessly eliminating it.

A commonplace example may help us to see this. Take the simple instance of a person who becomes hungry and eats. One might treat the hunger as a tendency and the eating as the act, and say that the hunger produces and explains the eating. Such an explanation seems patently true. Actually, it is a marked misrepresentation of what takes place. It omits the intervening process of self interaction through which the person moulds his act. Let us trace the hypothetical act. First, the person has to note his own hunger. If he didn't point it out to himself, he would be merely uncomfortable and restless and would not organize himself to search for food. Then he has to define his hunger in terms of whether it is something he should take care of. A glance at his watch may indicate that it is a half-hour before eating time and so he may decide to do nothing about it for that half hour. Or, he may remind himself that he is on a diet and say to himself, "too bad, you will just have to skip a meal," and thus not act at all on the basis of the hunger. Or he may decide that he will eat. If so, he has to engage further in constructing his act. Through the use of images he points out to himself various possibilities of action—the selection of different kinds of food, different sources of food, and different ways of getting to the food. In parading different food objects before his mind's eye, he may fashion an intention of having a very delectable meal. Then he may recall or point out to himself the depleted state of cash in his pocket and, accordingly, map out another line of action. He may take into consideration the weather, the inconvenience of going out of doors, the food in the refrigerator, or the reading that he wants to do. He may be decided as to what he is going to eat and be on his way to a given eating place, only to meet an acquaintance who invites him to have some drinks at the corner tavern. Because of some social obligation to the acquaintance, he may tell himself that the discreet thing to do, contrary to his wishes, is to accept the invitation. So the act which started off with a hungry tendency may end up with three hours of beer drinking.

Only a few of the many possibilities of lines of action are suggested in the illustration. But the illustration should suffice to remind us of what the slightest bit of self-observation would disclose, namely, that human action is built up through a process of self-indication. In this process the actor notes various things, defines and weighs them, projects out different possibilities of action, selects among them, makes decisions, and revises his plans as he takes account of something new. If anything is evident, it is that human action is not a sheer release of an already organized tendency or a mere matter of the tendency sweeping the individual along in a relentless move toward its realization. To the contrary, the actor has to piece together his line of action in the light of what he takes into account. In doing so, he acts back on his tendency, fitting it into the action which he is building up. In fitting his tendency into the developing act, he may organize it, transform it, hold it in suspense, block it, or sternly cast it aside as a basis of action.

We can appreciate more fully how inane is the idea that the tendency to act controls the act as soon as we think of the possible influence of the situation in which action is to take place or when we think of the effect of the activities of other people.

In a new and different situation a person has the need of carving out a new line of activity. He has to size up the situation, get cues, judge this or that, and piece together some line of activity that will enable him to fit the situation as he sees it. The situation will pose new demands and present new possibilities. By definition, these new demands and possibilities are not incorporated in the tendency which antedates them and which has been built up without regard to them. To presume under such conditions that a knowledge of the antecedent tendency will forecast the act that is to be built up in the new situation is presumptuous, indeed. Correspondingly, to presume that a knowledge of an attitude toward an object in one situation foretells action toward that object in a different kind of situation is to seriously misunderstand and misrepresent the nature of the human act.

An even more telling consideration against the idea that the tendency or attitude controls the act is the effect of the activities of others on one's own activity. As Mead has stressed, in group life one has to fit one's own act to the on-going activities of others. What one's associates are doing becomes the context inside of which one's own developing act has to fit. Thus, the expression by them of their expectations and intentions, their solicitations and instructions, their demands and commands are matters which the individual has to take into account in fashioning his own act. Now, obviously, one cannot foretell from a knowledge of the tendency what may be the acts of others that one may be called on to meet. Nor does a knowledge of the tendency spell out how the person is going to interpret those acts. The interpretation depends on how he sizes up the situation in which they occur. Particularly, in newly emerging situations wherein all of a given group are involved, the stream of definition and redefinition of one another's acts brings antecedent tendencies inside a crucible of dissolution.

I submit then that a realistic analysis of the human act shows that the tendency to act cannot be taken as moulding or controlling the act. At the best the tendency or preparation to act is merely an element that enters into the developing act—no more than an initial bid for a possible line of action. There are, of course, the relatively infrequent cases wherein the tendency seems to dominate the act to the exclusion of the demands of the situation and the expectations of others—cases such as mood of melancholy, the craving of a drug addict for narcotics, a burning rage, and fright in a panic. These are instances in which there is no process of self-indication, or, as we commonly say, instances in which the individual "loses his head." That such instances are not the prototype of human social action is quickly seen in the fact that they stand in opposition to group life. If everyone expressed freely his felt tendencies and attitudes, social life would become a state of anarchy. There would be no human group for sociologists to study.

The import of this analysis of the act is that what is crucial is not the tendency but the process by which the act is built up—not the attitude but the defining process through which the individual comes to forge his act. In the case of individual conduct this defining process is in the form of self-interaction, as the individual views the factors in his situation and takes into account the activities of others. In this process the individual indicates things to himself, defines them, judges them, prepares plans of action, chooses between them, and makes decisions. In the case of group or collective conduct it is in the form of social interaction wherein individuals define the acts of one another and mobilize themselves for collective action. Since the act, whether individual or collective, is fashioned, constructed, and directed by the process of definition that goes on in the individual or the group as the case may be, it is this process that should be the central object of study by the psychologist and the sociologist. A knowledge of this process would be of far greater value for prediction, if that is one's interest, than would any amount of knowledge of tendencies or attitudes. Yet this process is ignored in the current study of attitudes.

In the remaining portion of this paper I wish to consider briefly some other ways in which the concept of attitude is employed currently.

The term "attitude" may be employed as we use it in everyday life when we speak of a person having a mean attitude, or nurturing an attitude of suspicion, or having an intolerant attitude toward foreigners, or having a loving attitude toward his children. Several things should be noted about this usage. First, the term, "attitude," as such, adds nothing to comprehension; it could be omitted without any loss in meaning. We can communicate as effectively by saying that a person is suspicious as by saying that he has an attitude of suspicion, that he is intolerant of foreigners as that he has an intolerant attitude toward them, that he hates Jews as that he has an attitude of hatred toward them. The verb or the qualifying adjective or adverb is what is important and not the noun, "attitude." In such everyday usage—a usage which is carried into our scholarly literature—the term "attitude" becomes a convenient circumlocution but it is not necessary and has, in itself, no definite reference. Second, in this common usage, the term refers less to what the person will do and more to what sort of a state he is in. In learning that a person has an attitude of suspicion, of hatred, of love, or of indecision, we can take his role in some degree and thus catch something of his feelings, his sensitivities, and his point of view. This gives us some clue as to how he is disposed to handle that part of his world to which the attitude refers and this, in turn, serves to guide us in approaching and treating him. Third, this aid in taking the role of a person depends on how the attitude is characterized. A mere label, such as that the attitude is one of suspicion, enables us to take his role somewhat but not a great deal; an acute and penetrating description of his suspicion, such as a sensitive novelist might give, would permit us to take his role far more thoroughly and understandingly. To have a characterization structured along fixed and limited lines, as is necessarily true in the case of the results of attitude measurement studies, restricts the fullness to which one can take the role of the person.

In the study of human conduct, wherein human actors are carving out lines of action, it is of utmost importance to take their roles and get inside of their framework of operation. While, as I have said, the concept of attitude is not necessary to do this, its use as a means of facilitating role-taking is in order and may be helpful. We can note this in the justly famous work of Thomas and Znaniecki on the Polish Peasant when under the rubric of attitude they give us telling characterizations of the experiences of persons, as over against their untenable formal treatment of attitudes as supposed scientific concepts.

The one remaining way of using the concept of attitudes is to be found among some of the more thoughtful and cautious students engaged in attitude-measurement work. They make no claims that they are studying "attitudes" as commonly conceived, or that they are seeking to isolate tendencies to act, or that their findings can be used for predicting behavior or, indeed, that their procedure at the present stage is suited to the analysis of individual or group conduct. Instead, they regard their research in the measurement of so-called attitudes as purely exploratory without any prejudgment as to whether it may lead to a fruitful or meaningful scheme for the analysis of empirical conduct. They know that their devices catch something although they do not know what it is or what is its significance. They realize that this stable item is not subject to independent empirical study apart from revealing it through their devices. Thus, they recognize that they are in no position to say that it is a tendency to act or to ascribe generic characteristics to it. For them, the stable element is merely an exploratory tool to find out what use, if any, it may have. Thus, because of its quantitative nature, it may be correlated with other kinds of quantitative data. Or, since it allows for arrangement on a continuum it enables a comparison between different individuals or groups on such a continuum. Or, because of being a point allocation on a continuum it enables some determination of shifts on the continuum in response to the exposure of people to new kinds of experiences. They hope that such exploratory efforts *may* lead to the isolation of an empirical item with established generic characteristics—an item which thereby may become a scientific concept and an analytical tool.

Such exploratory study—like any kind of exploratory study in empirical science—is unquestionably in order. However, the concept of attitude which it presupposes can scarcely command approval. An attitude is made equivalent to the stable finding yielded by a given measurement study. Since the nature of this stable finding is unknown, the concept of attitude becomes, in turn, an unknown "X." This unsatisfactory state is made worse by the fact that the stable finding is limited to each given study instead of characterizing some universe of instances. Thus, in a strict logical sense, there is no concept of attitude in attitude-measurement studies. Instead, there is an endless array of separate so-called attitudes or "X's," with nothing to tie them together. This is indeed an odd form for an alleged scientific concept.

Enough has been said in this paper to suggest a genuine need to re-examine carefully our thought and our work in attitude study. Such an examination should lead thoughtful scholars in our field to grip their empirical world with more realistic and thoughtful tools.

5

Psychological Import
of the Human Group

The aim of this paper is to stress the need of respecting the nature of human group life in formulating social psychological theories and schemes of research. Such respect is lacking in contemporary social psychology to a far greater extent than is ordinarily realized. Most conceptions of the human group which are present today in our field are not formed through careful empirical study of human association, but are primarily projections of notions or schemes derived from other sources. This condition, in my judgment, is responsible for much of the confusion and difficulty which besets present-day social psychology. Faithful regard for the nature of human association would require, I suspect, the alteration and rejection of many ideas and practices which are stock in trade today among many social psychologists.

I take it for granted that the *raison d'être* of social psychology lies in the fact of human association. A *social* psychology must rest on the premise that the term "psychological," however conceived in content, has a character that arises from the association of human beings with one another. This fact, and only this fact, as far as I can see, distinguishes social psychology from other kinds of psychology.

From Group Relations at the Crossroads, *edited by Muzafer Sherif and M. O. Wilson. Copyright 1953 by Harper & Row, Publishers, Incorporated.*

Physiological psychology views its subject matter in terms of the organic structure of the individual and is concerned with the organization and functioning of nervous, muscular and glandular tissue. Individual psychology, in the traditional sense, takes the human being as a psychological entity who contains within himself the elements, factors or processes essential to his understanding. So regarded, the individual is analyzed both in composition and conduct without special regard to his association with his fellows. Social psychology, in contrast to physiological and individual psychology, accepts the fact of such association as its point of departure. The premise of social psychology is that group life is the setting inside of which individual experience takes place, and that such group life exerts a decisive influence on such experience. Its point of view reflects a recognition that association with his fellows is the universal and unavoidable lot of the human being; that such association constitutes an intricate network of stimulation in such forms as solicitations, demands, commands, prohibitions, incitations, rebuffs, expectations, condemnations and judgments by others; and that such a network of multiform actions of his associates gives form and structure to the psychological makeup of the individual. This is true whether the psychological referent be a total matter, such as so-called "personality," or some element, such as impulse, appetite, attitude or feeling, or some process such as cognition, motivation, learning or communication. From the social psychological point of view, all such items of reference have natures that arise out of the experience and happenings of human association. These few remarks are designed to underline the recognition that, logically, social psychology rests on the fact of human association.

This being true, it is necessary for social psychology to have a reasonably true picture of human association as its point of departure. Yet, instead of developing a scheme of the nature of human association through empirical observation, most social psychologists import their schemes, or manufacture schemes to accord with some preëstablished conception, or operate unwittingly with schemes that are dictated by their methods of study. I would like to justify this accusation.

It seems to me that there are four ways by which social psychologists arrive at their schemes of representing human association. The *first* way—one which is very common—is to start out with a given idea as to the psychological makeup of the human being and then construct a picture of the human group that will conform to this idea. Sometimes this occurs in the form of a direct assertion that group life is composed of the given psychological item; sometimes the assertion is absent, but a picture of group life is drawn that is congenial and compatible with the psychological item. The psychological literature shows many conceptions of human group life formed in these ways. An early instance was the doctrine of instincts. Starting from an idea that psychologically the human being was composed of a variety of instincts, students thought of group life or associative life as merely compounded out of such instincts. Thus, to take one familiar example: the institution of family life, which actually involves very complex and variable interaction between family members, was explained as an expression of a few chosen instincts, such as a combination of sex, parental, and gregarious instincts. Today such a conception seems grotesque in the light of the intricate, variable, and shifting complex of person-to-person adjustments that occur in family living. Yet this example from the field of instinct psychology reveals neatly how a conception or scheme of human group life may be built up merely by taking some presumed psychological character of the human individual and using it as the unit or "building block" of group life.

It would not be fair to rest my case by relying on the straw man of the now discarded instinct doctrine. So I will take contemporary examples. A very clear instance is given in the current doctrine of attitudes. Here we have a view which presumes that the human being consists of an organization of attitudes. Since it is reasoned that the human group consists of individuals, it is concluded that the life of the human group must consist of an interaction of the attitudes held by the constituent members. Accordingly, analysis of group behavior is undertaken to identify the attitudes which are supposed to give rise to such behavior. Indeed, the identification of such attitudes is conceived as supplying the firm basis for the prediction of group behavior. Later I will explain why I think that it is false to conceive of human association or group life as an interaction of attitudes. Here I merely wish to point out that this view, like the previous instinct conception, is a clear instance of forming a scheme of group life by an outward projection of some alleged psychological character of the human individual. Still other current instances of this same nature—instances which I will not spell out—are the conception of human group life as organized in terms of psychoanalytic factors, the notion that group life consists of a network of stimulus-response relations, the view that public opinion consists of a summation of individual opinions, and the view that group life, or any portion of it, such as a social movement, is an expression of individual motives, however these motives may be conceived.

Several things may be noted about this common way of schematizing human association in terms of some psychological attribute or makeup of the human individual. *First* is the fact that the picture or scheme of group life to which it leads is not developed from the empirical study of group life. Instead, the scheme is formed to accommodate an already established conception derived from an entirely different source. *Second*, such a way of schematizing group life leads to a vicious cycle which averts the fundamental task of social psychology. The conception of group life which is itself fashioned in terms of a given psychological character of the individual rebounds in an obvious circular manner to affirm the given psychological character. Thus the crucial requirement of a social psychology to approach the "psychological" through the "social" becomes short-circuited and aborted. In short, the conception of human association as a compound of the psychological makeup of the participating individuals becomes an obstacle to the study of such association. This is undeniably the most unfortunate consequence—a consequence which is always ready to plague social psychology and cut at its very roots.

A *second* major way of arriving at a guiding image or picture of human association is to use an analogical construct. The human group is given a form or nature by likening it to something else. Frequently, this analogy is made unwittingly as a by-product of some metaphysical scheme which the student is employing. Examples of both these modes of analogy in social psychology are many. The witting and deliberate method of entertaining analogical conceptions of the human group is well illustrated by what sociologists refer to as the "organic analogy." Here the human group is conceived as formed in the pattern of an organism, functioning as an entity and guiding the behavior of its subgroups and ultimately of the individual members. Interaction between the members becomes merely instrumental to the unified action of the group. Another instance of this analogical approach was the former effort to conceive of group life in terms of a group mind, with the group mind being endowed with the functional characteristics of the mind of the individual. More common today in social psychology is the unwitting employment of analogy in forging a conception of the human group, usually in the service of some metaphysical or methodological scheme. Thus if a social psychologist commits himself to regard his object of study as a mechanism operating in orderly and regularized fashion, then his operating scheme of human association will be cast in such a mold. Or, if the social psychologist follows a methodological approach which presupposed that his object of study exists in the form of a statistical aggregate operating on a probability basis, then he will be led to an implied scheme of human association that answers to this approach. Or, if he holds the conception of "Gestalt" philosophy to the effect that any and all objects of study exist in the form of total systems seeking to achieve or maintain a state of equilibrium, then this conception will be imparted to his scheme of the human group. In all of these instances it is clear that a scheme of human association is fabricated either wittingly or unwittingly on the basis of analogy, by presuming that human association has a structure or character like that of some given outside model. If you recognize, as I am sure you do, that the models commonly employed by social psychologists are patterned after those in the natural sciences or organized in accordance with some philosophical conception, then you can understand how a form is fastened on human association that does not come from the empirical study of such association. Since this particular source of schematizing the human group is tied in so definitely with the very act of scientific research, it is easy to see how marked is the resort by social psychologists to analogical procedure in developing functioning conceptions of human association. I am not interested at this point in commenting on the validity of any of these analogical constructs of the human group; I wish merely to note again that they represent schemes that are importations instead of being formed through empirical study.

There is a *third* way by which operating schemes of the fundamental nature of the human group are performed. This is to develop a general conception of the human group not on the basis of analogical reasoning, but on the basis of speculative reflection. This approach is most conspicuous in the case of political philosophers, particularly as they develop guiding ideas as to the nature of the State in relation to society. It is evident in views such as that society is "general will" or "power." It is perhaps most familiar to social psychologists in the sociological concept of "consensus." Social psychologists from the sociological field have been frequently guided by this conception. It is a conception based on speculative reflection—not on careful empirical observation. Since, on the whole, views of human association derived from such speculative reflection are not too common among contemporary social psychologists, I will not dwell on this matter. It is sufficient to note that this way of schematizing the nature of the human group avoids the inductive study which is necessary for the emergence of a realistic conception.

The *fourth* and final way by which conceptions of human association are reached is through empirical studies of human groups, such as have been made especially by anthropologists and sociologists. The conceptions derived in this manner that are most conspicuous today in the field of social psychology center around the terms "culture," "social structure," and "role playing." Because of their prominence in current social psychological thought these conceptions might be discussed briefly. The accumulation over the past century of a vast body of information on the ways of living of diverse human groups has given rise to the concept of culture. Such information shows decisively that ways of group living vary independently of ethnic makeup, geographical setting, or the particular composition of the people. In fact, the ways of living are seemingly products of historical experience. The information shows, further, that the ways of living in any given group, granted that the group has some continuity and stability, persist rather tenaciously from generation to generation, thus being impressed on the young and channelizing their activity. These observations gave rise easily to a notion of culture, or a conception of the human group as having a body or system of ways of living which antedate the infant or newcomer, which must be acquired by the infant or newcomer, and which shape their conduct and personal organization. Evidence in support of this conception is so voluminous that it is easy to see how students would come to regard human group life as cultural life. (Some sociologists even define their discipline as the science of culture.)

Adjacent to this conception of culture, and indeed supplementary to it, are the notions of the human group as a social structure and as a system of social roles. The study of the social organization of human groups shows always an arrangement of social positions, whether they be conceived in terms of a division of labor or in terms of a hierarchy of status. It is to be noted, further, that each one of these positions is socially defined by expectations as to how the occupant is to act and be socially valued in relation to other positions. In this way the conception of the human group as culture merges with the conception of the group as social structure. Similarly tied in is the conception of group life as role playing. This latter notion, like that of culture and social structure, is based on empirical study. It refers to the obvious fact that the human being in his relations to others is put into or adopts different roles—father, worker, scholar, husband, friend, enemy, leader, wealthy man, loyal adherent, teacher, officer of a club, and so on, depending on the social position of the individual and his lines of pursuit. It would seem that whenever one human being enters into relationship with another he immediately falls into some sort of role, and that as long as he is in relationship he will be in one role or another. It is easy to see how students would reach the notion that human group life is role playing.

Indeed, the empirical evidence on behalf of the idea that culture, social structure, and role playing constitute the human group and its life seems so compelling that we need not be surprised to notice how influential is this conception in contemporary social psychology. Yet, despite the fact that any instance of settled group life or human association will show the undeniable presence of cultural norms or patterns, status positions and role playing, in my judgment it is inadequate, erroneous, and distorting to regard these three items as constituting the human group or as representing the nature of human association. The proof for this assertion will be given later in this paper. Here I merely wish to point out that the conceptions of culture, social structure, and role playing have not been derived from the study of human association as an on-going process. Rather, they have been formed through the study of certain products of human association. I make these statements quite seriously. The conceptions have not been reached through a careful study of what happens between people who are engaged in interaction with each other. Instead, these conceptions were formed by the comparison of group ways of living, or through the observation of relationships, or through noting the differentiated positions or parts taken by individuals in the context of the group. To conceive of human association in terms of culture, status position, and role playing is actually to employ imported conceptions. What seem, superficially, to be empirically derived conceptions of the nature of human association turn out not to be derived from the study of association as such.

From this brief survey of the four major ways by which contemporary social psychologists usually arrive at their schemes of the nature of human association or of the human group, one may perceive a little more clearly the meaning of my original assertion that present-day social psychology suffers both in not having and in not seeking a realistic conception of the nature of human association. To build up conceptions of human association on the basis of accommodating some philosophical notion or some scheme of research methodology, or on the basis of some philosophical speculation on human group life, or, finally, on the basis of empirical observation of the human group, which however is not observation of association as such, is to avoid the crucial problem of social psychology. As I sought to show in my earlier remarks, social psychology is required by logical necessity to take its point of departure from the fact of human association. Social psychology should have, and I think must have, a faithful picture of that association in order to develop a realistic understanding of its world of concern. This is necessary, irrespective of how such a realistic picture would affect present forms of thought and inquiry and irrespective of where such a picture would lead social psychology.

I want to say something now about the nature of human association. Human association should be viewed in its most fundamental form, namely, that of two human beings interacting upon each other. The larger instances of human association, such as we have in mind in talking about group life in its wider aspects, are still based on interaction between individuals. So the initial and strategic point of study is the interaction between individuals. I intend to consider only a few, yet crucial, features of such interaction, omitting many others which are important but which need not be considered in this paper. The features that I will discuss are empirical—you should be able to note them quickly in observing interaction around you.

In my judgment, the most important feature of human association is that the participants *take each other into account*. While this statement may seem to be redundant and innocuous, I think that in reality it is crucial. Taking another person into account means more than merely being in his presence or merely responding to him. Two individuals asleep in a bed may respond to each other as they shift in their sleeping postures; however, they are not taking each other into account in such responses. Taking another person into account means being aware of him, identifying him in some way, making some judgment or appraisal of him, identifying the meaning of his action, trying to find out what he has on his mind or trying to figure out what he intends to do. Such awareness of another person in this sense of taking him and his acts into consideration becomes the occasion for orienting oneself and for the direction of one's own conduct. One takes the other person and his action into account not merely at the point of initial contact, but actually throughout the period of interaction. One has to keep abreast of the action of the other, noting what he says at this point and that point or interpreting his movements as they appear, one after another. Perceiving, defining and judging the other person and his action and organizing oneself in terms of such definitions and judgments constitute a continuing or running process.

The fact that *each* of the two individuals in our simple situation is taking the other into continuing account is very important. It means that the two individuals are brought into a relation of *subject to subject,* not of object to object, nor even of subject to object. Each person has to view the conduct of the other in some degree from the standpoint of the other. One has to catch the other as a subject, or in terms of his being the initiator and director of his acts; thus one is led to identify what the person means, what are his intentions and how he may act. Each party to the interaction does this and thus not only takes the other into account, but takes him into account as one who, in turn, is taking him into account. This relation of subject to subject introduces a responsiveness into the interaction which is quite different from the formal responsiveness between two objects. Taking each other into account in this mutual way not only relates the action of each to that of the other but intertwines the actions of both into what I would call, for lack of a better word, a transaction —a fitting of the developing action of each into that of the other to form a joint or overbridging action. Without going astray along esoteric lines I would say that the transaction is something other than an addition of the actions of the two individuals; these two lines of action in their developing interrelationship constitute a singleness, such as we recognize when we speak of an argument, a debate, a discussion or a fight.

Next, we should note that the transaction (which I think is the real form of human interaction) is constructed or built up in the process of its occurrence, and is thus subject to having a variable career. Human interaction flows on in a movement of definition and redefinition of one another's action. It is built up from point to point as each takes the other into account again and again and is similarly taken into account by the other. Each participant in the face of a given expression of action of the other must note and judge the expression and use it as a factor for guiding his own action. This imparts to the transaction a developing character as it passes from one definition to another and depends on the selections, judgments and decisions that are made. This picture of human association as a flowing process in which each participant is guiding his action in the light of the action of the other suggests its many potentialities for divergent direction.

Yet, except on relatively infrequent occasions, human group life is not noticeably instable or irregular. The prevalence of relatively ordered and stable human group life in face of the fact that such group life is constantly being built up brings to light the controls that enter into the development of a transaction. The very fact of taking another into account becomes a control over one's own developing act. One has to mobilize oneself in terms of how one has taken the other into account. But how one takes account of the other—that is, identifies and interprets the action of the other—is not predetermined by that action. The interpretation depends instead on the schemes of definition which the individual possesses and on the nature of his own act in terms of his purposes, aims or directions. His schemes of definitions incorporate the definitions of his fellows, i.e., the expectations of how one should act in a given situation. They may also incorporate schemes of his own as they have been forged in his experience. In both cases they introduce order and continuity into how he defines the action of the other, and thus they function as controls over his own action. Yet it must be borne in mind that in response to his own developing act he may exercise selection between the schemes of definition which he has, or, rather, he may define his own definition and thus take the action of the other person into account in a different way.

To introduce a fuller measure of sense into what I have just said, I find it necessary to say something about another crucial aspect of human association, namely, that the participant not only interacts with the other person but interacts with himself. In being aware of another, in interpreting and judging his action and in identifying him in a given way, one is making indications to oneself. Indeed, it seems that only by virtue of making an indication to oneself can one take account of something as distinguished from merely responding to that thing. One directs one's attention to the thing, holds it before him, suspends during that time his overt action toward the thing, inspecting it, analyzing it and making a judgment of it. This self-interaction, whatever we may wish to call it, takes place inside of the interaction with the other person and becomes the means whereby one's own act becomes mobilized and organized in that interaction. I do not wish to make any analysis of what is involved in the interaction of the human being with himself. George Herbert Mead has sketched what I think are the basic features of this self-interaction in his classic discussion of the relation between the "I" and the "Me." Apparently it is through this self-interaction that the human group in its larger aspects, or what Mead calls the community, enters into the interaction between human beings, even though that group or community is not physically present in the interaction. In making indications to himself the human being may apply to his conduct the norms of the perspectives of the group and thus guide himself in interaction with others by considerations which are not immediately present in that interaction.

The final aspect of human interaction that I wish to note is that the participants are required by necessity to inhibit tendencies to act. Inclinations, impulses, wishes and feelings may have to be restrained in the light of what one takes into account and in the light of how one judges or interprets what one takes into account. The presence of the other and his developing acts become occasions for the orientation of one's own act and thus provide the incidents of experience which lead one as he is guiding his own action to check himself at this point or that point, to withhold expression of given feelings and to recognize that certain wishes must be held in abeyance.

My remarks about the nature of human interaction are sketchy and probably none too clear. But they are sufficient to suggest what I think all of us can see, namely, that human association is a moving process in which the participants note and gauge each other's actions, each organizing his action with regard to the other and, in doing so, inhibiting himself, encouraging himself, and guiding himself as he builds up his action. With such a rudimentary scheme in mind I would like to return to a consideration of the schemes of human association in current social psychology and make some assessment of them.

First, it seems clear that it is improper to conceive human association in terms of a given psychological character or composition of the individual human being. Human association is a flowing and developing process in which the act of each individual becomes organized, bent, redirected or built up in the light of how he takes others into account. The makeup of the individual, as well as elements of that makeup, comes under the influence of the developing interaction, being withheld at this point, suppressed at others, and revised at others. The makeup and the elements are subject to the restraints and reorganizations that come from fitting action into the action of others. Because of the fact that interaction is a process having the character and results that have been noted, it seems logically necessary to recognize that it cannot be legitimately construed in terms of some hypothecated scheme of the psychological makeup of the human being. To illustrate the point I will use a single example among the many current schemes of group life that are formed out of some idea of the psychological makeup of the human being. I have in mind the widespread view that human association is an interaction of attitudes—a view which is deeply entrenched in current social psychological thought and study. This view posits that individual behavior is an expression of the attitudes of the individual; hence, since the group represents an association of individuals, the behavior present in that association stems from attitudes possessed by the participants. Such a scheme of group life ignores the fact and nature of association itself. It is an inadequate and false view. If scrutinized in terms of what has been said regarding features of human association, any psychological element like attitude should be easily recognized as merely having a place in the developing process of interaction and as coming under the control of

112

that process. Thus, as one takes account of the developing acts of others, attitudes may be mobilized, or they may be scrupulously suppressed or held in abeyance, or they may be given a new twist, or they may be sapped in their vigor as one's own act becomes incorporated into new stable forms of association that are built up, or they may be rendered nonfunctional in that the actions of the others, as interpreted, provide no occasion for their expression. A soldier may have a profound antipathy or so-called antagonistic attitude toward the lieutenant of his platoon, yet he may obey all of his orders and be reasonably polite in his conduct toward that lieutenant; he may temper his attitude by some feeling of shared pride as the lieutenant is congratulated by an inspecting officer on the efficiency of the platoon; and he may even make some significant sacrifice on behalf of the lieutenant in the heat of battle. The point is that, in the flowing sequence of interpretation of the actions of others, one in developing his own act subjects his so-called attitudes to highly variable use or disuse. The vital dependency of the attitude on the nature of the on-going interaction suggests how fallacious it is to use the attitude to construct the scheme of that interaction. Yet I need not remind you how widespread is the view today that individual and group conduct is to be understood and predicted in terms of attitudes despite the fact that such conduct is built up through associative interaction.

This assessment of human group life as an interaction of attitudes applies equally well to any other of the numerous schemes which seek to construe human association in terms of some projected psychological character of the human individual. There is a beguiling temptation to social psychologists to reason that, since the human group is composed of individuals, the life of the group must be composed of what are regarded as the psychological elements of the individuals. Yet it is precisely at this point that a social psychologist may go astray and become unrealistic by failing to see and understand that interaction constitutes the group life, and that such interaction must be viewed in its own terms.

To turn now to the analogical schemes which represent a second way of conceiving the nature of human association, I suspect that practically all of them are questionable when judged in terms of the features of human association spoken of above. Thus the likening of human group life to the operation of a mechanical structure, or to the functioning of an organism, or to a system seeking to achieve equilibrium, seems to me to face grave difficulties in view of the formative and explorative character of interaction as the participants judge each other and guide their own acts by that judgment. Let me use one of these analogical schemes for illustrative comment— that used occasionally in "Gestalt" psychology. The idea that the conduct of an individual in a group setting is a vector created and coerced by the stresses of that setting, as it moves to a state of equilibrium, amounts essentially in my judgment to a denial of the role of definition, assessment, sizing up or decision in the guidance of one's own act vis-à-vis the developing actions of other participants. I find it hard to conceive that those of you who at this moment judge my remarks as erroneous are pressed to that judgment by an operative tendency of our group situation to move toward homeostasis; I suspect, rather, that in taking my remarks into account you are dissecting them, trying to ascertain their meaning, judging them and organizing yourself in regard to them in diverse ways—in ways that may set a problem for unity in our subsequent discussion but which at the present are not expressions of a system seeking to reach equilibrium. The human being is not swept along as a neutral and indifferent unit by the operation of a system. As an organism capable of self interaction he forges his action out of a process of definition involving choice, appraisal and decision.

In view of the ease with which an analogical scheme of human group life may shape forms of study and analysis it is important, I think, to square the scheme with the observable character of human group life.

Nothing must be said here about the third general way of framing a conception of the nature of human group life which I discussed above, namely, the reliance on philosophical speculation as to that nature. This approach suffers from the failure to study in close detail what takes place in human association.

I wish, however, to dwell somewhat on the fourth way of arriving at a conception of the nature of the human group as I have discussed it above. I have in mind the notions that the human group is an organization of culture and social positions, with the behavior of the participants being a playing of roles. These notions are admittedly derived through some empirical observation of group life, yet they do not stand up well, in my judgment, when scrutinized in the light of a careful analysis of human association. If one takes a given instance of associative interaction, such as is taking place between us, one must readily admit the presence of a so-called culture, social structure and playing of roles. Thus in our relations we are unquestionably guided by various "cultural" norms, such as for you to listen to my remarks with reasonable quiet and for me to speak and, in doing so, to respect a code of what is proper and allowable before a scholarly audience. Also, there is something in the nature of a social structure in our relationship, partially in terms of status positions and positions of authority and respect and partially in terms of a division of labor. Further, there is no question that we play many roles in our relationship—roles as university professors, as scholars, as critics, as polite and dignified individuals and as guests. Yet I would submit that, after we apply in the most exhaustive manner possible these schemes of cultural norms, social positions and social roles, we would miss what is most vital in our interaction, namely, the presentation of my ideas and your judgment and assessment of them. If any of you were to try to convey a reasonably intelligent picture of what is occurring to some one of your friends who is not present, you would give a sorry account if you limited yourself to a listing of the cultural norms which we are following or to a characterization of our social positions and our roles. At best, such an account would yield only an idea of a formal setting. It would obviously fail to catch my views, their meaning, your interpretation and assessment of them, and my own handling of your expressed judgments as I may be confronted with them in discussion. It seems to me evident, although I suspect that here I stand apart from my sociological brethren, that one cannot realistically squeeze the process of human interaction into the mold of culture, social structure, and role playing. There are cases of human association which are heavily ritualized, as in a stylized religious ceremony, wherein each overt action of each participant is definitely prescribed at each given point, with the total interaction involving the taking account of one another only in terms of such prescriptions. Here the fit of the conceptions of culture, social structure, and role playing approximates perfection. But such instances are relatively infrequent in human group life and should not be used as the prototype of human group life. Human group life is a process of formative transaction. Cultural norms, status positions and role relationships are only frameworks inside of which that process goes on.

Enough has been said, I hope, to indicate that the association of human beings has certain features that give it its peculiar character. These features should be faithfully respected in any scheme to study human group life empirically. The development of a realistic social psychology is especially dependent on an empirically valid picture of the nature of human association. The perspective of social psychology, its manner of setting problems, its modes of inquiry, and its lines of analysis are set logically by the fact of the "social." If the "social" is framed in terms of some scheme which is fictitious in whole or in part, inquiry will be shunted into false channels and analysis made in false ways. Unfortunately in my opinion, present-day social psychology is relying to a formidable extent on schemes of human association which do not reflect faithfully the nature of that association. A false picture of the human group leads to a false picture of how the individual human being is formed by participating in group life. It leads to erroneous proposals of how human beings, individually and collectively, can be changed, and thus it affects vitally questions of social policy. In these days when there is increased solicitation of social psychologists to study problems of practical import and to offer recommendations as to lines of action, it becomes more important than ever for social psychologists to be realistically oriented. I believe that for social psychologists such realistic orientation must come initially and chiefly through an accurate representation of the nature of human association.

6

An Appraisal
of Thomas and Znaniecki's
The Polish Peasant
in Europe and America

To form a proper perspective of the study made by Thomas and Znaniecki, one must realize that it is not a mere monograph on Polish peasant society. It is primarily an attempt to lay the basis for scientific social research and for scientific social theory. This attempt is based on four considerations.

1. They desire to construct an approach that is adapted to the character of life in a complex civilized society. Particularly, it must be suited to the study of social change and transformation since this feature is outstanding in such a society. Further, the approach must be such as to lead to social theory adequate for social control.

To appreciate this point, it should be realized that there may be forms of study which do not have this character. Indeed, much of present day social research, however scientifically imposing, is not suited to the study of a changing society. Further, much of it may yield findings and relations which are "precise" without being able to offer any knowledge as to *how to change or control these relations*. This indicates that such research is not being applied to the line of inquiry which the theoretical character of social life requires.

Herbert Blumer, "An Appraisal of Thomas and Znaniecki's The Polish Peasant in Europe and America." *Reprinted from Social Science Council Bulletin 44,* Critiques of Research in the Social Sciences: I (1939), pp. 69–81.

The ultimate test of the validity of scientific knowledge is the ability to use it for purposes of social control.

A scheme for the scientific study of social life must be able to cope with the central character of social life, and must offer the possibility of yielding knowledge that can be used for the control of that social life. The authors have endeavored to construct such a scheme.

2. A second consideration is the need of an approach that fits the unique character of change or interaction as it occurs in the case of human social life. What is unique, according to Thomas and Znaniecki, is the presence of a subjective as well as an objective factor. The influence of any objective factor always is dependent on the selective receptivity and positive inclination of the person. And, correspondingly, the change of an objective factor (as far as its influence on persons is concerned) is dependent upon the application to it of a new point of view or orientation. It is this idea which, as we have seen, the authors have expressed in their declaration that both objective setting and subjective experience must be taken into account in the study of social change. It is this idea which they have expressed in their basic concepts of attitude and value, and it is this idea which they have elaborated and extended to their methodological formula designed to yield "laws of social becoming."

It seems certain that this methodological formula is invalid and that the thought of securing "laws of becoming" by it is chimerical. Further, one may even question both the logical and methodological adequacy of the concepts of "attitude" and "value." These admissions, however, do not affect the validity of the general belief that social life involves the interaction of objective factors and subjective experience. This notion, indeed, is in accord with common sense; it might be expressed in the statement that an individual acts toward objects in terms of what they mean to him.

An adequate scheme for the study of human society must pay due attention to this subjective factor. This, Thomas and Znaniecki have consistently sought to do, by always keeping an eye on human experience. They regard approaches which ignore or omit this subjective factor and which merely study relations between objective factors as being necessarily deficient, and incapable of yielding adequate knowledge of social life. Such approaches, it should be noted, are very conspicuous in contemporary social research and are usually justified and fortified by assertions as to their objectivity and scientific character.

3. The third consideration springs from the one just mentioned. It is a realization of the need of devising means that will enable one to "catch" this subjective factor and study it in interaction with the objective factor. This is an inescapable need if one admits the role of the subjective factor. The authors have faced the problem squarely. Their answer, as we have seen, is that the means are provided by "human documents." The human document as an account of human experience gives empirical data on the subjective factor. Further, it is an "objective" record, enabling others to have access to the data and permitting one to return always to them.

4. The final consideration is the realization of the need of a theoretical framework in order to study social life. An approach without a guiding scheme is no approach. In the case of their own scheme, it should be noted that it is constructed on the basis of the very factors which represent the uniqueness of social life and which logically constitute the fact of social change. These factors are the subjective and objective as they are involved in interaction. As we have seen, the authors have conceptualized these factors in their notion of attitudes and values, and, with these as the foundation stones, they have developed the theoretical framework which we have considered. Their interest, in other words, has been to develop a conceptual scheme that would permit one to handle analytically and abstractly concrete material on social life, and thus permit comparative studies of different societies.

It is with a methodological scheme organized around these considerations that Thomas and Znaniecki made their monographic study of Polish peasant society. The scheme is well organized on the logical and methodological sides; the authors show full familiarity with the logic of science and with the canons of scientific procedure.

The application of the scheme to the Polish peasant society is a trial—in the sense of both an exemplification and a test. The authors are engaged in a pioneer undertaking; they continually stress the need of comparable studies of other societies to verify the "laws" and generalizations arrived at in the study of the Polish peasant; and in their concluding remarks* they emphasize the tentative character of their method, their analyses, and their results.

In the absence of comparable studies of other societies which can serve as a test of the authors' generalizations and theories, we are not in a position to decide categorically on their truth or falsity. All that can be done is to consider critically the application of their methodological approach (their "standpoint and method") to the study of the Polish peasant society. Since this application centers in the analysis of an extensive body of materials by means of a series of theoretical schemes, our interest must be focused on this undertaking. As a result, we have to ignore consideration of the rich body of illuminating interpretations which the authors have made of the Polish peasant society.

The problem, then, which confronts us here is that of the relation between their materials and their theoretical analysis. This problem has arisen at a number of points in our previous discussion; here we must consider it again. It is a problem which lies at the heart of the authors' undertaking; and it is a problem which is central in all social research which seeks to get at the "subjective" factor by means of documentary material, for it is a problem, ultimately, as to whether social research into subjective experience can be made to be scientific.

As we have seen, Thomas and Znaniecki, cognizant of the need of getting material on the subjective factor, have advocated the use of "human documents," of which they regard the life record as the most perfect form. They have given a vast quantity of various human documents in their work. These documentary materials are admittedly not as satisfactory as they would wish, but were the best that they could secure. These materials are those on which their work is primarily based, in the sense that supposedly the theoretical analyses either arose out of them or were tested by them. What can be said on this point of their inductive character? How does one work

---

* "Our work does not pretend to give any definite and universally valid sociological truths, nor to constitute a permanent model of sociological research; it merely claims to be a monograph, as nearly complete as possible under the circumstances, of a limited social group at a certain period of its evolution, which may suggest studies of other groups, more detailed and more perfect methodically, thus helping the investigation of modern living societies to rise above its present stage of journalistic impressionism, and preparing the ground for the determination of really exact general laws of human behavior." (Vol. II, 1822–23)

with human documents? How does one analyze them and interpret them?

It seems quite clear that Thomas and Znaniecki did not derive all of their theoretical conceptions from the materials which are contained in their volumes or from similar materials which they did not put into their volumes. Perhaps not even the major theoretical conceptions were derived from them. Indeed, the major outlines are foreshadowed in the previous writings of Thomas. It is rather self-evident that the authors began their study of the Polish peasant with the rudiments of their primary theoretical schemes, built out of much experience with human beings, many reflections and observations on human conduct, and considerable appreciation of human nature. Only individuals with such experience and gifts could have made the stimulating and incisive interpretations that they have made. It is further self-evident that their *particular* interpretations of Polish peasant life were not formed solely from the materials they present; we have to assume that the familiarity with Polish peasant life which enabled their interpretations was made in a wide variety of ways. Thus, while there can be no question but that much of the theoretical conception of the authors came from handling the documents, it is also true that a large part of it did not.

This point, in itself, is not important, except that it explains why the theoretical conceptions in *The Polish Peasant* far exceed the materials. The authors have shown surprising liberality in making generalizations—generalizations which seem to be very good, but for which there are few if any data in the materials. Omitting this overload of generalization, the important question is whether the materials adequately test the generalizations (regardless of their source) which are being applied to the materials. As our previous discussion has pointed out, the answer is very inconclusive. Some interpretations, indeed, are borne out by the content of the documents, and sometimes the interpretations do not seem to be verified adequately; in both instances, of course, the materials are a test. Usually, however, one cannot say that the interpretation is either true or not true, even though it is distinctly plausible.

In instances of plausible interpretations, all that one can say is that the interpretation makes the materials more significant than they were and makes the theoretical interpretation more understandable and familiar than it was previously. Perhaps, this is all that one can expect or should expect in the interpretative analysis of human documentary material. It is just this which one finds to be true of *The Polish Peasant,* yet if the theoretical analysis of human documents either only can be, or should be, of this sort, it leaves behind a number of important considerations and problems.

1. First, it would mean, obviously, that the materials are not a decisive test of the theoretical interpretations. Yet, the fact that both the material and the interpretation acquire significance and understanding that they did not have before, seems to mean that it is not a mere case of the illustration of the theory.

2. Second, it would follow that the test of the validity of such theory would have to come in other ways, such as in its internal consistency, in the character of its assumptions, in its relation to other theories, in its consistency with what seems to be "human," or in other kinds of data than those provided by human documents.

3. Third, it would seemingly imply that the essential function of human documents would be to provide human materials which would yield to a sensitive and inquiring mind hunches, insights, questions suitable for reflection, new perspectives, and new understandings.

These considerations seem to represent the way in which the authors have actually worked with their theoretical conceptions and their data. In the authors, we have two excellent minds with a rich experience with human beings, with a keen sensitivity to the human element in conduct, with some fundamental notions and interests, with a number of important problems, with a variety of hunches, with a lively curiosity and sense of inquiry, with a capacity for forming abstract concepts—two minds, of this sort, approaching voluminous accounts of human experience, mulling over them, reflecting on them, perceiving many things in them, relating these things to their background of experience, checking these things against one another, and charting all of them into a coherent abstract and analytical pattern. Perhaps, this is, after all, how the scientist works. At any rate, it is not surprising that out of such efforts, Thomas and Znaniecki should have produced such an impressive work as this analysis of Polish peasant society.

In the light of the general discussion of *The Polish Peasant,* some concluding thoughts may be given on the problem of the scientific analysis of human documents.

It seems clear that the meaningful content of such documents is dependent on the ideas, questions, and knowledge with which their analysis is undertaken. While this is true, obviously, in the understanding of any body of scientific materials, it seems to be more pronounced in the interpretation of records of human experience. Such a record is less self-evident as to its meaning. The implication is that, generally, the value of the analysis will depend on the experience, intelligence, skill, and fruitful questions of the student. As these factors vary, so will vary the interpretation. The person who has a broad acquaintance with human beings, who, as we say popularly, understands human nature, and who has an intimate familiarity with the area of experience that he is studying, should make a more able analysis than one who is less well equipped in these respects. This, of course, is to be expected. The point is worthy of mention here only to emphasize that the interpretative content of a human document depends markedly on the competence and theoretical framework with which the document is studied. One person, by virtue of his experience and his interests, may detect things in a document that another person would not see.

The flexibility of a document to interpretation would be of no importance if the document could be used as an effective test of the specific interpretation which is made of it, but it is at this point that difficulty·enters. In the case of simple facts, the document may indeed prove or disprove an assertion made about it, but the closer one approaches to abstract interpretation the less satisfactory is the document as a test. Human documents seem to lend themselves readily to diverse interpretations. One can see this in the ease with which they can be analyzed by different theories of motivation. Theories seem to order the data.

The reasons for this condition may be sought, presumably, in a number of directions. One reason which readily suggests itself is that the document may not be sufficiently thorough: what is needed is a fuller and more ample account of the experience which is interpreted. Many students of social research hold to this belief and, accordingly, have committed themselves to the meritorious task of securing "exhaustive" accounts. Thomas and Znaniecki have this idea in mind in advocating the use of "life histories." Theoretically, an exhaustive account which would present all details of an experience or series of experiences would serve as a decisive test of interpretation. Actually, such exhaustive accounts are not secured and, perhaps, never can be secured. In the case of accounts which are generally regarded as being full and detailed (as in the autobiography of Wladek or in a psychoanalytic record), one still finds an inability of the account to test decisively most interpretations. The interpretation may be plausible and even self-evident to one who holds the theory from which the interpretation stems; to another who has a different theoretical framework, a different interpretation may seem to be more telling and true.

This suggests that the deficiency of human documents as a test of interpretation is due in large part to the nature of the act of interpretation. To interpret is to apply concepts or categories, and it seems that such interpretation in the instance of the human document, as in that of any human experience, is so much a matter of judgment that categories that are congenial and self-evident to one, readily fit the experience.* Perhaps, this need not always be true; it does seem, however, to represent the present status of the interpretation of human experience, especially so, on the more abstract levels.

It would follow that the validation or invalidation of many theories and views has to be done by means other than the use of *specific experiences*. Such means as those of logical criticism, relation to other theories and bodies of fact, and the use of a mass of general experiences (as is done in supporting the theory of culture as against the doctrine of instinct) seem to be those which are commonly employed. Specific accounts of experience serve, apparently, only to make clear the nature of the interpretation. The point suggested here (as applied to human documents) may be stated extremely in the declaration that a document has value only in terms of the theory with which it is interpreted, but that the validity of the theory usually cannot be determined by the document.

One way in which students may attempt to test the interpretation of human documents is by the use of statistical procedure. This procedure would consist of the collection of a representative number of accounts and the determination of the proportion that show the given interpretation. This would be compared with a control group.

* Part of the difficulty comes from the fact that the categories employed are left undefined, or else are defined in an imprecise manner. Consequently, one is at a loss to identify details of experience that would permit one to determine whether or not the category fits. The application of the category is a matter of judicious judgment rather than of decisive test.

Such a procedure, however, while methodologically sound, would be of no special value if the separate documents, whether of the study group or of the control group, could not be used as an effective test of the interpretation.

This whole situation suggests something in the nature of a dilemma. On one hand, the study of social life seems to require the understanding of the factor of human experience. This subjective aspect must be secured, as Thomas and Znaniecki show. Studies which confine themselves to "objective factors" remain inadequate and one-sided. Yet the identification of the human experience or subjective factor, seemingly, is not made at present in ways which permit one to test crucially the interpretation. Identification and interpretation remain a matter of judgment. Their acceptance depends on their plausibility. At best, the materials only enable one to make out a *case* for the theoretical interpretation.

The inadequacy of human documents in testing interpretation is a primary reason why they are rejected by many as materials for scientific study. When one adds to this the fact that usually the separate document cannot very well stand evaluation according to the criteria of representativeness, adequacy, and reliability, it is easy to see why human documents become suspect as a scientific instrument. Yet to renounce their use in the scientific investigation of human life would be to commit a fatal blunder, for theoretically, they are indispensable and actually they may be of enormous value. The effective use which has been made of them by Thomas and Znaniecki is ample demonstration of this value.

A few concluding remarks may be made on this point. First, one should note that human documents may be very serviceable in aiding the student to acquire an intimate acquaintance with the kind of experience he is studying, in suggesting leads, in enabling insight, and in helping him to frame more fruitful questions. It is much better to develop one's theoretical judgments with the aid of such documents than to form them, speaking extremely, in a vacuum. The use of documents offers to the student the opportunity to increase his experience and to sharpen his sense of inquiry. Other things being equal, the student who develops through the use of documents an intimate acquaintance with an area of life will be able to analyze it more fruitfully than would one lacking such an acquaintance.

In a sense, human documents serve the reader of a report in the same way in which they serve the investigator. They permit him to form a closer acquaintance with the kind of experience which is being studied and to form a judgment as to the reasonable nature of the proposed interpretations. Admittedly, this judgment will vary with different readers; those who possess a facility in understanding human beings and who already have an intimate familiarity with the people being studied can make a better judgment than those lacking this facility and this intimate knowledge. Perhaps, only the judgments of those who are similar or superior in competence and familiarity to the investigator are significant in the critical evaluation of a report. Other readers would have to temper their own judgments by some acceptance, on authority, of the analysis which the investigator makes of human documents.

7

Sociological Analysis and the "Variable"*

M y aim in this paper is to examine critically the scheme of sociological analysis which seeks to reduce human group life to variables and their relations. I shall refer to this scheme, henceforth, as "variable analysis." This scheme is widespread and is growing in acceptance. It seems to be becoming the norm of proper sociological analysis. Its sophisticated forms are becoming the model of correct research procedure. Because of the influence which it is exercising in our discipline, I think that it is desirable to note the more serious of its shortcomings in actual use and to consider certain limits to its effective application. The first part of my paper will deal with the current shortcomings that I have in mind and the second part with the more serious question of the limits to its adequacy.

SHORTCOMINGS IN CONTEMPORARY
VARIABLE ANALYSIS

The first shortcoming I wish to note in current variable analysis in our field is the rather chaotic condition that prevails in the selec-

* Presidential address read at the annual meeting of the American Sociological Society, September, 1956.

Herbert Blumer, "Sociological Analysis and the 'Variable'," Vol. XXII (1956), reprinted by permission of The American Sociological Review *and the American Sociological Association.*

tion of variables. There seems to be little limit to what may be chosen or designated as a variable. One may select something as simple as a sex distribution or as complex as a depression; something as specific as a birth rate or as vague as social cohesion; something as evident as residential change or as imputed as a collective unconscious; something as generally recognized as hatred or as doctrinaire as the Oedipus complex; something as immediately given as a rate of newspaper circulation to something as elaborately fabricated as an index of anomie. Variables may be selected on the basis of a specious impression of what is important, on the basis of conventional usage, on the basis of what can be secured through a given instrument or technique, on the basis of the demands of some doctrine, or on the basis of an imaginative ingenuity in devising a new term.

Obviously the study of human group life calls for a wide range of variables. However, there is a conspicuous absence of rules, guides, limitations and prohibitions to govern the choice of variables. Relevant rules are not provided even in the thoughtful regulations that accompany sophisticated schemes of variable analysis. For example, the rule that variables should be quantitative does not help, because with ingenuity one can impart a quantitative dimension to almost any qualitative item. One can usually construct some kind of a measure or index of it or develop a rating scheme for judges. The proper insistence that a variable have a quantitative dimension does little to lessen the range or variety of items that may be set up as variables. In a comparable manner, the use of experimental design does not seemingly exercise much restriction on the number and kind of variables which may be brought within the framework of the design. Nor, finally, does careful work with variables, such as establishing tests of reliability, or inserting "test variables," exercise much restraint on what may be put into the pool of sociological variables.

In short, there is a great deal of laxity in choosing variables in our field. This laxity is due chiefly to a neglect of the careful reduction of problems that should properly precede the application of the techniques of variable analysis. This prior task requires thorough and careful reflection on the problem to make reasonably sure that one has identified its genuine parts. It requires intensive and extensive familiarity with the empirical area to which the problem refers. It requires a careful and thoughtful assessment of the theoretical schemes that might apply to the problem. Current variable analysis in our field is inclined to slight these requirements both in practice and in the training of students for that practice. The scheme of variable analysis has become for too many just a handy tool to be put to immediate use.

A second shortcoming in variable analysis in our field is the disconcerting absence of generic variables, that is, variables that stand for abstract categories. Generic variables are essential, of course, to an empirical science—they become the key points of its analytical structure. Without generic variables, variable analysis yields only separate and disconnected findings.

There are three kinds of variables in our discipline which are generally regarded as generic variables. None of them, in my judgment, is generic. The first kind is the typical and frequent variable which stands for a class of objects that is tied down to a given historical and cultural situation. Convenient examples are: attitudes toward the Supreme Court, intention to vote Republican, interest in the United Nations, a college education, army draftees and factory unemployment. Each of these variables, even though a class term, has substance only in a given historical context. The variables do not stand directly for items of abstract human group life; their application to human groups around the world, to human groups in the past, and to conceivable human groups in the future is definitely restricted. While their use may yield propositions that hold in given cultural settings, they do not yield the abstract knowledge that is the core of an empirical science.

The second apparent kind of generic variable in current use in our discipline is represented by unquestionably abstract sociological categories, such as "social cohesion," "social integration," "assimilation," "authority," and "group morale." In actual use these do not turn out to be the generic variables that their labels would suggest. The difficulty is that such terms, as I sought to point out in an earlier article on sensitizing concepts,* have no fixed or uniform indicators. Instead, indicators are constructed to fit the particular problem on which one is working. Thus, certain features are chosen to represent the social integration of cities, but other features are used to represent the social integration of boys' gangs. The indicators chosen to represent morale in a small group of school

---

* "What Is Wrong with Social Theory?" *American Sociological Review*, 19 (February 1954), 3–10.

children are very different from those used to stand for morale in a labor movement. The indicators used in studying attitudes of prejudice show a wide range of variation. It seems clear that indicators are tailored and used to meet the peculiar character of the local problem under study. In my judgment, the abstract categories used as variables in our work turn out with rare exception to be something other than generic categories. They are localized in terms of their content. Some measure of support is given to this assertion by the fact that the use of such abstract categories in variable research adds little to generic knowledge of them. The thousands of "variable" studies of attitudes, for instance, have not contributed to our knowledge of the abstract nature of an attitude; in a similar way the studies of "social cohesion," "social integration," "authority," or "group morale" have done nothing, so far as I can detect, to clarify or augment generic knowledge of these categories.

The third form of apparent generic variable in our work is represented by a special set of class terms like "sex," "age," "birth rate," and "time period." These would seem to be unquestionably generic. Each can be applied universally to human group life; each has the same clear and common meaning it its application. Yet, it appears that in their use in our field they do not function as generic variables. Each has a content that is given by its particular instance of application, e.g., the birth rate in Ceylon, or the sex distribution in the State of Nebraska, or the age distribution in the City of St. Louis. The kind of variable relations that result from their use will be found to be localized and non-generic.

These observations on these three specious kinds of generic variables point, of course, to the fact that variables in sociological research are predominantly disparate and localized in nature. Rarely do they refer satisfactorily to a dimension or property of abstract human group life. With little exception they are bound temporally, spatially, and culturally and are inadequately cast to serve as clear instances of generic sociological categories. Many would contend that this is because variable research and analysis are in a beginning state in our discipline. They believe that with the benefit of wider coverage, replication, and the co-ordination of separate studies disparate variable relations may be welded into generic relations. So far there has been little achievement along these lines. Although we already have appreciable accumulations of findings from variable studies, little has been done to convert the findings into generic relations. Such conversion is not an easy task. The difficulty should serve both as a challenge to the effort and an occasion to reflect on the use and limitations of variable analyses.

As a background for noting a third major shortcoming I wish to dwell on the fact that current variable analysis in our field is operating predominantly with disparate and not generic variables and yielding predominantly disparate and not generic relations. With little exception its data and its findings are "here and now," wherever the "here" be located and whenever the "now" be timed. Its analyses, accordingly, are of localized and concrete matters. Yet, as I think logicians would agree, to understand adequately a "here and now" relation it is necessary to understand the "here and now" context. This latter understanding is not provided by variable analysis. The variable relation is a single relation, necessarily stripped bare of the complex of things that sustain it in a "here and now" context. Accordingly, our understanding of it as a "here and now" matter suffers. Let me give one example. A variable relation states that reasonably staunch Erie County Republicans become confirmed in their attachment to their candidate as a result of listening to the campaign materials of the rival party. This bare and interesting finding gives us no picture of them as human beings in their particular world. We do not know the run of their experiences which induced an organization of their sentiments and views, nor do we know what this organization is; we do not know the social atmosphere or code in their social circles; we do not know the reinforcement and rationalizations that come from their fellows; we do not know the defining process in their circles; we do not know the pressures, the incitants, and the models that came from their niches in the social structure; we do not know how their ethical sensitivities are organized and so what they would tolerate in the way of shocking behavior on the part of their candidate. In short, we do not have the picture to size up and understand what their confirmed attachment to a political candidate means in terms of their experience and their social context. This fuller picture of the "here and now" context is not given by variable relations. This, I believe, is a major shortcoming in variable analysis, insofar as variable analysis seeks to explain meaningfully the disparate and local situations with which it seems to be primarily concerned.

The three shortcomings which I have noted in current variable research in our field are serious but perhaps not crucial. With increasing experience and maturity they will probably be successfully overcome. They suggest, however, the advisability of inquiring more deeply into the interesting and important question of how well variable analysis is suited to the study of human group life in its fuller dimensions.

LIMITS OF VARIABLE ANALYSIS

In my judgment, the crucial limit to the successful application of variable analysis to human group life is set by the process of interpretation or definition that goes on in human groups. This process, which I believe to be the core of human action, gives a character to human group life that seems to be at variance with the logical premises of variable analysis. I wish to explain at some length what I have in mind.

All sociologists—unless I presume too much—recognize that human group activity is carried on, in the main, through a process of interpretation or definition. As human beings we act singly, collectively, and societally on the basis of the meanings which things have for us. Our world consists of innumerable objects—home, church, job, college education, a political election, a friend, an enemy nation, a tooth brush, or what not—each of which has a meaning on the basis of which we act toward it. In our activities we wend our way by recognizing an object to be such and such, by defining the situations with which we are presented, by attaching a meaning to this or that event, and where need be, by devising a new meaning to cover something new or different. This is done by the individual in his personal action, it is done by a group of individuals acting together in concert, it is done in each of the manifold activities which together constitute an institution in operation, and it is done in each of the diversified acts which fit into and make up the patterned activity of a social structure or a society. We can and, I think, must look upon human group life as chiefly a vast interpretative process in which people, singly and collectively, guide themselves by defining the objects, events, and situations which they encounter. Regularized activity inside this process results from the application of stabilized definitions. Thus, an institution carries on its complicated activity through an articulated complex of such stabilized meanings. In the face of new situations or new experiences individuals, groups, institutions and societies find it necessary to form new definitions. These new definitions may enter into the repertoire of stable meanings. This seems to be the characteristic way in which new activities, new relations, and new social structures are formed. The process of interpretation may be viewed as a vast digestive process through which the confrontations of experience are transformed into activity. While the process of interpretation does not embrace everything that leads to the formation of human group activity and structure, it is, I think, the chief means through which human group life goes on and takes shape.

Any scheme designed to analyze human group life in its general character has to fit this process of interpretation. This is the test that I propose to apply to variable analysis. The variables which designate matters which either directly or indirectly confront people and thus enter into human group life would have to operate through this process of interpretation. The variables which designate the results or effects of the happenings which play upon the experience of people would be the outcome of the process of interpretation. Present-day variable analysis in our field is dealing predominantly with such kinds of variables.

There can be no doubt that, when current variable analysis deals with matters or areas of human group life which involve the process of interpretation, it is markedly disposed to ignore the process. The conventional procedure is to identify something which is presumed to operate on group life and treat it as an independent variable, and then to select some form of group activity as the dependent variable. The independent variable is put at the beginning part of the process of interpretation and the dependent variable at the terminal part of the process. The intervening process is ignored or, what amounts to the same thing, taken for granted as something that need not be considered. Let me cite a few typical examples: the presentation of political programs on the radio and the resulting expression of intention to vote; the entrance of Negro residents into a white neighborhood and the resulting attitudes of the white inhabitants toward Negroes; the occurrence of a business depression and the resulting rate of divorce. In such instances—so common to variable analysis in our field—one's concern is with the two variables and not with what lies between them. If one has neutralized other factors which are regarded as possibly exercising influence on the dependent variable, one is content with the conclusion that the observed change in the dependent variable is the necessary result of the independent variable.

This idea that in such areas of group life the independent variable automatically exercises its influence on the dependent variable is, it seems to me, a basic fallacy. There is a process of definition intervening between the events of experience presupposed by the independent variable and the formed behavior represented by the dependent variable. The political programs on the radio are interpreted by the listeners; the Negro invasion into the white neighborhood must be defined by the whites to have an effect on their attitudes; the many events and happenings which together constitute the business depression must be interpreted at their many points by husbands and wives to have any influence on marital relations. This intervening interpretation is essential to the outcome. It gives the meaning to the presentation that sets the response. Because of the integral position of the defining process between the two variables, it becomes necessary, it seems to me, to incorporate the process in the account of the relationship. Little effort is made in variable analysis to do this. Usually the process is completely ignored. Where the process is recognized, its study is regarded as a problem that is independent of the relation between the variables.

The indifference of variable analysis to the process of interpretation is based apparently on the tacit assumption that the independent variable predetermines its interpretation. This assumption has no foundation. The interpretation is not predetermined by the variable as if the variable emanated its own meaning. If there is anything we do know, it is that an object, event or situation in human experience does not carry its own meaning; the meaning is conferred on it.

Now, it is true that in many instances the interpretation of the object, event or situation may be fixed, since the person or people may have an already constructed meaning which is immediately applied to the item. Where such stabilized interpretation occurs and recurs, variable analysis would have no need to consider the interpretation. One could merely say that as a matter of fact under given conditions the independent variable is followed by such and such a change in the dependent variable. The only necessary precaution would be not to assume that the stated relation between the variables was necessarily intrinsic and universal. Since anything that is defined may be redefined, the relation has no intrinsic fixity.

Alongside the instances where interpretation is made by merely applying stabilized meanings there are the many instances where the interpretation has to be constructed. These instances are obviously increasing in our changing society. It is imperative in the case of such instances for variable analysis to include the act of interpretation in its analytic scheme. As far as I can see, variable analysis shuns such inclusion.

Now the question arises, how can variable analysis include the process of interpretation? Presumably the answer would be to treat the act of interpretation as an "intervening variable." But, what does this mean? If it means that interpretation is merely an intervening neutral medium through which the independent variable exercises its influence, then, of course, this would be no answer. Interpretation is a formative or creative process in its own right. It constructs meanings which, as I have said, are not predetermined or determined by the independent variable.

If one accepts this fact and proposes to treat the act of interpretation as a formative process, then the question arises how one is to characterize it as a variable. What quality is one to assign to it, what property or set of properties? One cannot, with any sense, characterize this act of interpretation in terms of the interpretation which it constructs; one cannot take the product to stand for the process. Nor can one characterize the act of interpretation in terms of what enters into it—the objects perceived, the evaluations and assessments made of them, the cues that are suggested, the possible definitions proposed by oneself or by others. These vary from one instance of interpretation to another and, further, shift from point to point in the development of the act. This varying and shifting content offers no basis for making the act of interpretation into a variable.

Nor, it seems to me, is the problem met by proposing to reduce the act of interpretation into component parts and work with these parts as variables. These parts would presumably have to be processual parts—such as perception, cognition, analysis, evaluation, and

135

decision-making in the individual; and discussion, definition of one another's responses and other forms of social interaction in the group. The same difficulty exists in making any of the processual parts into variables that exist in the case of the complete act of interpretation.

The question of how the act of interpretation can be given the qualitative constancy that is logically required in a variable has so far not been answered. While one can devise some kind of a "more or less" dimension for it, the need is to catch it as a variable, or set of variables, in a manner which reflects its functioning in transforming experience into activity. This is the problem, indeed dilemma, which confronts variable analysis in our field. I see no answer to it inside the logical framework of variable analysis. The process of interpretation is not inconsequential or pedantic. It operates too centrally in group and individual experience to be put aside as being of incidental interest.

In addition to the by-passing of the process of interpretation there is, in my judgment, another profound deficiency in variable analysis as a scheme for analyzing human group life. The deficiency stems from the inevitable tendency to work with truncated factors and, as a result, to conceal or misrepresent the actual operations in human group life. The deficiency stems from the logical need of variable analysis to work with discrete, clean-cut and unitary variables. Let me spell this out.

As a working procedure variable analysis seeks necessarily to achieve a clean identification of the relation between two variables. Irrespective of how one may subsequently combine a number of such identified relations—in an additive manner, a clustering, a chain-like arrangement, or a "feedback" scheme—the objective of variable research is initially to isolate a simple and fixed relation between two variables. For this to be done each of the two variables must be set up as a distinct item with a unitary qualitative make-up. This is accomplished first by giving each variable, where needed, a simple quality or dimension, and second by separating the variable from its connection with other variables through their exclusion or neutralization.

A difficulty with this scheme is that the empirical reference of a true sociological variable is not unitary or distinct. When caught in its actual social character, it turns out to be an intricate and inner-moving complex. To illustrate, let me take what seems ostensibly to be a fairly clean-cut variable relation, namely between a birth control program and the birth rate of a given people. Each of these two variables—the program of birth control and the birth rate—can be given a simple discrete and unitary character. For the program of birth control one may choose merely its time period, or select some reasonable measure such as the number of people visiting birth control clinics. For the birth rate, one merely takes it as it is. Apparently, these indications are sufficient to enable the investigator to ascertain the relations between the two variables.

Yet, a scrutiny of what the two variables stand for in the life of the group gives us a different picture. Thus, viewing the program of birth control in terms of *how it enters into the lives of the people*, we need to note many things such as the literacy of the people, the clarity of the printed information, the manner and extent of its distribution, the social position of the directors of the program and of the personnel, how the personnel act, the character of their instructional talks, the way in which people define attendance at birth control clinics, the expressed views of influential personages with reference to the program, how such personages are regarded, and the nature of the discussions among people with regard to the clinics. These are only a few of the matters which relate to how the birth control program might enter into the experience of the people. The number is sufficient, however, to show the complex and inner-moving character of what otherwise might seem to be a simple variable.

A similar picture is given in the case of the other variable—the birth rate. A birth rate of a people seems to be a very simple and unitary matter. Yet, in terms of what it expresses and stands for in group activity it is exceedingly complex and diversified. We need consider only the variety of social factors that impinge on and affect the sex act, even though the sex act is only one of the activities that set the birth rate. The self-conceptions held by men and by women, the conceptions of family life, the values placed on children, accessibility of men and women to each other, physical arrangements in the home, the sanctions given by established institutions, the code of manliness, the pressures from relatives and neighbors, and ideas of what is proper, convenient and tolerable in the sex act—these are a few of the operating factors in the experience of the group that play upon the sex act. They suffice to indicate something of the complex

137

body of actual experience and practice that is represented in and expressed by the birth rate of a human group.

I think it will be found that, when converted into the actual group activity for which it stands, a sociological variable turns out to be an intricate and inner-moving complex. There are, of course, wide ranges of difference between sociological variables in terms of the extent of such complexity. Still, I believe one will generally find that the discrete and unitary character which the labeling of the variable suggests vanishes.

The failure to recognize this is a source of trouble. In variable analysis one is likely to accept the two variables as the simple and unitary items that they seem to be, and to believe that the relation found between them is a realistic analysis of the given area of group life. Actually, in group life the relation is far more likely to be between complex, diversified and moving bodies of activity. The operation of one of these complexes on the other, or the interaction between them, is both concealed and misrepresented by the statement of the relation between the two variables. The statement of the variable relation merely asserts a connection between abbreviated terms of reference. It leaves out the actual complexes of activity and the actual processes of interaction in which human group life has its being. We are here faced, it seems to me, by the fact that the very features which give variable analysis its high merit—the qualitative constancy of the variables, their clean-cut simplicity, their ease of manipulation as a sort of free counter, their ability to be brought into decisive relation—are the features that lead variable analysis to gloss over the character of the real operating factors in group life, and the real interaction and relations between such factors.

The two major difficulties faced by variable analysis point clearly to the need for a markedly different scheme of sociological analysis for the areas in which these difficulties arise. This is not the occasion to spell out the nature of this scheme. I shall merely mention a few of its rudiments to suggest how its character differs fundamentally from that of variable analysis. The scheme would be based on the premise that the chief means through which human group life operates and is formed is a vast, diversified process of definition. The scheme respects the empirical existence of this process. It devotes itself to the analysis of the operation and formation of human group life as these occur through this process. In doing so it seeks to trace the lines of defining experience through which ways of living, patterns of relations, and social forms are developed, rather than to relate these formations to a set of selected items. It views items of social life as articulated inside moving structures and believes that they have to be understood in terms of this articulation. Thus, it handles these items not as discrete things disengaged from their connections but, instead, as signs of a supporting context which gives them their social character. In its effort to ferret out lines of definition and networks of moving relation, it relies on a distinctive form of procedure. This procedure is to approach the study of group activity through the eyes and experience of the people who have developed the activity. Hence, it necessarily requires an intimate familiarity with this experience and with the scenes of its operation. It uses broad and interlacing observations and not narrow and disjunctive observations. And, may I add, that like variable analysis, it yields empirical findings and "here-and-now" propositions, although in a different form. Finally, it is no worse off than variable analysis in developing generic knowledge out of its findings and propositions.

In closing, I express a hope that my critical remarks about variable analysis are not misinterpreted to mean that variable analysis is useless or makes no contribution to sociological analysis. The contrary is true. Variable analysis is a fit procedure for those areas of social life and formation that are not mediated by an interpretative process. Such areas exist and are important. Further, in the area of interpretative life variable analysis can be an effective means of unearthing stabilized patterns of interpretation which are not likely to be detected through the direct study of the experience of people. Knowledge of such patterns, or rather of the relations between variables which reflect such patterns, is of great value for understanding group life in its "here-and-now" character and indeed may have significant practical value. All of these appropriate uses give variable analysis a worthy status in our field.

In view, however, of the current tendency of variable analysis to become the norm and model for sociological analysis, I believe it important to recognize its shortcomings and its limitations.

8

What Is Wrong
with Social Theory?*

My concern is limited to that form of social theory which stands
or presumes to stand as a part of empirical science.†

The aim of theory in empirical science is to develop analytical
schemes of the empirical world with which the given science is concerned. This is done by conceiving the world abstractly, that is, in
terms of classes of objects and of relations between such classes.

* Paper read at the annual meeting of the American Sociological Society,
August, 1953.

† There are two other legitimate and important kinds of social theory which
I do not propose to assess. One of them seeks to develop a meaningful interpretation of the social world or of some significant part of it. Its aim is not
to form scientific propositions but to outline and define life situations so that
people may have a clearer understanding of their world, its possibilities of
development, and the directions along which it may move. In every society,
particularly in a changing society, there is a need for meaningful clarification of
basic social values, social institutions, modes of living and social relations. This
need cannot be met by empirical science, even though some help may be gained
from analysis made by empirical science. Its effective fulfillment requires a
sensitivity to new dispositions and an appreciation of new lines along which
social life may take shape. Most social theory of the past and a great deal in
the present is wittingly or unwittingly of this interpretative type. This type of
social theory is important and stands in its own right.

A second type of theory might be termed "policy" theory. It is concerned

*Herbert Blumer, "What Is Wrong with Social Theory?" Vol. XIX (1954),
reprinted by permission of The American Sociological Review and the American Sociological Association.*

Theoretical schemes are essentially proposals as to the nature of such classes and of their relations where this nature is problematic or unknown. Such proposals become guides to investigation to see whether they or their implications are true. Thus, theory exercises compelling influence on research—setting problems, staking out objects and leading inquiry into asserted relations. In turn, findings of fact test theories, and in suggesting new problems invite the formulation of new proposals. Theory, inquiry and empirical fact are interwoven in a texture of operation with theory guiding inquiry, inquiry seeking and isolating facts, and facts affecting theory. The fruitfulness of their interplay is the means by which an empirical science develops.

Compared with this brief sketch of theory in empirical science, social theory in general shows grave shortcomings. Its divorcement from the empirical world is glaring. To a preponderant extent it is compartmentalized into a world of its own, inside of which it feeds on itself. We usually localize it in separate courses and separate fields. For the most part it has its own literature. Its lifeline is primarily exegesis—a critical examination of prior theoretical schemes, the compounding of portions of them into new arrangements, the translation of old ideas into a new vocabulary, and the occasional addition of a new notion as a result of reflection on other theories. It is remarkably susceptible to the importation of schemes from outside its own empirical field, as in the case of the organic analogy, the evolutionary doctrine, physicalism, the instinct doctrine, behaviorism, psychoanalysis, and the doctrine of the conditioned reflex. Further, when applied to the empirical world social theory is primarily an interpretation which orders the world into its mold, not a studious cultivation of empirical facts to see if the theory fits. In terms of both origin and use social theory seems in general not to be geared into its empirical world.

---

with analyzing a given social situation, or social structure, or social action as a basis for policy or action. It might be an analysis of communist strategy and tactics, or of the conditions that sustain racial segregation in an American city, or of the power play in labor relations in mass production industry, or of the morale potential of an enemy country. Such theoretical analysis is not made in the interests of empirical science. Nor is it a mere application of scientific knowledge. Nor is it research inquiry in accordance with the canons of empirical science. The elements of its analysis and their relations have a nature given by the concrete situation and not by the methods or abstractions of empirical science. This form of social theorizing is of obvious importance.

Next, social theory is conspicuously defective in its guidance of research inquiry. It is rarely couched in such form as to facilitate or allow directed investigation to see whether it or its implications are true. Thus, it is gravely restricted in setting research problems, in suggesting kinds of empirical data to be sought, and in connecting these data to one another. Its divorcement from research is as great as its divorcement from its empirical world.

Finally, it benefits little from the vast and ever growing accumulation of "facts" that come from empirical observation and research inquiry. While this may be due to an intrinsic uselessness of such facts for theoretic purposes, it also may be due to deficiency in theory.

These three lines of deficiency in social theory suggest that all that is needed is to correct improper preoccupations and bad working practices in theorizing. We hear repeatedly recommendations and injunctions to this effect. Get social theorists to reduce drastically their preoccupation with the literature of social theory and instead get in touch with the empirical social world. Let them renounce their practice of taking in each other's washing and instead work with empirical data. Let them develop their own conceptual capital through the cultivation of their own empirical field instead of importing spurious currency from alien realms. Get them to abandon the practice of merely interpreting things to fit their theories and instead test their theories. Above all, get them to cast their theory into forms which are testable. Have them orient their theory to the vast bodies of accumulated research findings and develop theory in the light of such findings.

These are nice injunctions to which all of us would subscribe. They do have a limited order of merit. But they neither isolate the problem of what is basically wrong with social theory nor do they provide means of correcting the difficulties. The problem continues to remain in the wake of studies made with due respect to the injunctions. There have been and there are many able and conscientious people in our field, alone, who have sought and are seeking to develop social theory through careful, sometimes meticulous preoccupation with empirical data—Robert E. Park, W. I. Thomas, Florian Znaniecki, Edwin Sutherland, Stuart Dodd, E. W. Burgess, Samuel Stouffer, Paul Lazarsfeld, Robert Merton, Louis Wirth, Robin Williams, Robert Bales and dozens of others who equally merit mention.

142

All of these people are empirically minded. All have sought in their respective ways to guide research by theory and to assess their theoretical propositions in the light of empirical data. Practically all of them are familiar with the textbook canons of empirical research. We cannot correctly accuse such people of indifference to the empirical world, or of procedural naivete, or of professional incompetence. Yet their theories and their work are held suspect and found wanting, some theories by some, other theories by others. Indeed, the criticisms and countercriticisms directed to their respective work are severe and box the compass. It is obvious that we have to probe deeper than the level of the above injunctions.

In my judgment the appropriate line of probing is with regard to the concept. Theory is of value in empirical science only to the extent to which it connects fruitfully with the empirical world. Concepts are the means, and the only means of establishing such connection, for it is the concept that points to the empirical instances about which a theoretical proposal is made. If the concept is clear as to what it refers, then sure identification of the empirical instances may be made. With their identification, they can be studied carefully, used to test theoretical proposals and exploited for suggestions as to new proposals. Thus, with clear concepts theoretical statements can be brought into close and self-correcting relations with the empirical world. Contrariwise, vague concepts deter the identification of appropriate empirical instances, and obscure the detection of what is relevant in the empirical instances that are chosen. Thus, they block connection between theory and its empirical world and prevent their effective interplay.

A recognition of the crucial position of concepts in theory in empirical science does not mean that other matters are of no importance. Obviously, the significance of intellectual abilities in theorizing, such as originality and disciplined imagination, requires no highlighting. Similarly, techniques of study are of clear importance. Also, bodies of fact are necessary. Yet, profound and brilliant thought, an arsenal of the most precise and ingenious instruments, and an extensive array of facts are meaningless in empirical science without the empirical relevance, guidance and analytical order that can come only through concepts. Since in empirical science everything depends on how fruitfully and faithfully thinking intertwines with the empirical world of study, and since concepts are the gateway to that world, the effective functioning of concepts is a matter of decisive importance.

Now, it should be evident that concepts in social theory are distressingly vague. Representative terms like mores, social institutions, attitudes, social class, value, cultural norm, personality, reference group, social structure, primary group, social process, social system, urbanization, accommodation, differential discrimination and social control do not discriminate cleanly their empirical instances. At best they allow only rough identification, and in what is so roughly identified they do not permit a determination of what is covered by the concept and what is not. Definitions which are provided to such terms are usually no clearer than the concepts which they seek to define. Careful scrutinizing of our concepts forces one to recognize that they rest on vague sense and not on precise specification of attributes. We see this in our common experience in explaining concepts to our students or outsiders. Formal definitions are of little use. Instead, if we are good teachers we seek to give the sense of the concept by the use of a few apt illustrations. This initial sense, in time, becomes entrenched through the sheer experience of sharing in a common universe of discourse. Our concepts come to be taken for granted on the basis of such a sense. It is such a sense and not precise specifications that guides us in our discipline in transactions with our empirical world.

This ambiguous nature of concepts is the basic deficiency in social theory. It hinders us in coming to close grips with our empirical world, for we are not sure what to grip. Our uncertainty as to what we are referring obstructs us from asking pertinent questions and setting relevant problems for research. The vague sense dulls our perception and thus vitiates directed empirical observation. It subjects our reflection on possible relations between concepts to wide bands of error. It encourages our theorizing to revolve in a separate world of its own with only tenuous connection with the empirical world. It limits severely the clarification and growth that concepts may derive from the findings of research. It leads to the undisciplined theorizing that is bad theorizing.

If the crucial deficiency of social theory, and for that matter of our discipline, is the ambiguous nature of our concepts, why not proceed to make our concepts clear and definite? This is the nub of the problem. The question is how to do this. The possible lines of answer can be reduced a lot by recognizing that a great deal of endeavor, otherwise conscientious and zealous, does not touch the problem. The clarification of concepts is not achieved by introducing a new vocabulary of terms or substituting new terms—the task is not one of lexicography. It is not achieved by extensive reflection on theories to show their logical weaknesses and pitfalls. It is not accomplished by forming or importing new theories. It is not achieved by inventing new technical instruments or by improving the reliability of old techniques—such instruments and techniques are neutral to the concepts on behalf of which they may be used. The clarification of concepts does not come from piling up mountains of research findings. As just one illustration I would point to the hundreds of studies of attitudes and the thousands of items they have yielded; these thousands of items of findings have not contributed one iota of clarification to the concept of attitudes. By the same token, the mere extension of research in scope and direction does not offer in itself assurance of leading to clarification of concepts. These various lines of endeavor, as the results themselves seem abundantly to testify, do not meet the problem of the ambiguous concept.

The most serious attempts to grapple with this problem in our field take the form of developing fixed and specific procedures designed to isolate a stable and definitive empirical content, with this content constituting the definition or the reference of the concept. The better known of these attempts are the formation of operational definitions, the experimental construction of concepts, factoral analysis, the formation of deductive mathematical systems and, although slightly different, the construction of reliable quantitative indexes. Although these attempts vary as to the kind of specific procedure that is used, they are alike in that the procedure is designed to yield through repeated performances a stable and definitive finding. A definition of intelligence as being the intelligence quotient is a convenient illustration of what is common to these approaches. The intelligence quotient is a stable and discriminating finding that can be checked through a repetition of clearly specified procedures. Ignoring questions as to the differential merit and the differential level of penetration between these approaches, it would seem that in yielding a specific and discriminating content they are the answer to the problem of the ambiguous concept in social theory. Many hold that resolute employment of one or the other of these methods will yield definitive concepts with the consequence that theory can be applied decisively to the empirical world and tested effectively in research inquiry.

So far, the suitability of these precision endeavors to solving the problem of the ambiguous concept remains in the realm of claim and promise. They encounter three pronounced difficulties in striving to produce genuine concepts related to our empirical world.

First, insofar as the definitive empirical content that is isolated is regarded as constituting by itself the concept (as in the statement that, "X is the intelligence quotient") it is lacking in theoretic possibilities and cannot be regarded as yielding a genuine concept. It does not have the abstract character of a class with specifiable attributes. What is "intelligence quotient" as a class and what are its properties? While one can say that "intelligence quotient" is a class made up of a series of specific intelligence quotients, can one or does one point out common features of this series—features which, of course, would characterize the class? Until the specific instances of empirical content isolated by a given procedure are brought together in a class with common distinguishing features of content, no concept with theoretic character is formed. One cannot make proposals about the class or abstraction or relate it to other abstractions.

Second, insofar as the definitive empirical content that is isolated is regarded as qualifying something beyond itself (as in the statement that, "Intelligence is the intelligence quotient" wherein intelligence would now be conceived as including a variety of common sense references such as ability to solve business problems, plan campaigns, invent, exercise diplomatic ingenuity, etc.), the concept is constituted by this something which is beyond the definitive empirical content. But since this "something beyond" is not dealt with by the procedure yielding the definitive empirical content, the concept remains in the ambiguous position that originally set the problem. In other words, the concept continues to be constituted by general sense or understanding and not by specification.

Third, a pertinent question has to be faced as to the relation of the definitive empirical content that is isolated, to the empirical world that is the concern of the discipline. One has to have the possibilities of establishing the place and role of the specific content in the empirical world in order for the empirical content to enter into theory about the world. A specific procedure may yield a stable finding, sometimes necessarily so by the internal mechanics of the procedure. Unless this finding is shown to have a relevant place in the empirical world under study, it has no value for theory. The showing of such relevancy is a critical difficulty confronting efforts to establish definitive concepts by isolating stable empirical contents through precise procedures. Incidentally, the establishment of such relevancy is not accomplished by making correlations. While classes of objects or items covered by concepts may be correlated, the mere establishment of correlations between items does not form concepts or, in other words, does not give an item as an instance of a class, a place or a function. Further, the relevance of an isolated empirical content to the empirical world is not established merely by using the concept to label given occurrences in that empirical world. This is a semantic pit into which scores of workers fall, particularly those working with operational definitions of concepts or with experimental construction of concepts. For example, a careful study of "morale" made in a restricted experiment may yield a stable finding; however, the mere fact that we customarily label many instances in our empirical world with the term, "morale," gives no assurance, whatsoever, that such an experimental construct of "morale" fits them. Such a relation has to be established and not presumed.

Perhaps these three difficulties I have mentioned may be successfully solved so that genuine definitive concepts of theoretic use can be formed out of the type of efforts I have been considering. There still remains what I am forced to recognize as the most important question of all, namely whether definitive concepts are suited to the study of our empirical social world. To pose such a question at this point seems to move in a reverse direction, to contradict all that I have said above about the logical need for definitive concepts to overcome the basic source of deficiency in social theory. Even though the question be heretical I do not see how it can be avoided. I wish to explain why the question is very much in order.

I think that thoughtful study shows conclusively that the concepts of our discipline are fundamentally sensitizing instruments. Hence, I call them "sensitizing concepts" and put them in contrast with definitive concepts such as I have been referring to in the foregoing discussion. A definitive concept refers precisely to what is common to a class of objects, by the aid of a clear definition in terms of attributes or fixed bench marks. This definition, or the bench marks, serve as a means of clearly identifying the individual instance of the class and the make-up of that instance that is covered by the concept. A sensitizing concept lacks such specification of attributes or bench marks and consequently it does not enable the user to move directly to the instance and its relevant content. Instead, it gives the user a general sense of reference and guidance in approaching empirical instances. Whereas definitive concepts provide prescriptions of what to see, sensitizing concepts merely suggest directions along which to look. The hundreds of our concepts—like culture, institutions, social structure, mores, and personality—are not definitive concepts but are sensitizing in nature. They lack precise reference and have no bench marks which allow a clean-cut identification of a specific instance, and of its content. Instead, they rest on a general sense of what is relevant. There can scarcely be any dispute over this characterization.

Now, we should not assume too readily that our concepts are sensitizing and not definitive merely because of immaturity and lack of scientific sophistication. We should consider whether there are other reasons for this condition and ask particularly whether it is due to the nature of the empirical world which we are seeking to study and analyze.

I take it that the empirical world of our discipline is the natural social world of every-day experience. In this natural world every object of our consideration—whether a person, group, institution, practice or what not—has a distinctive, particular or unique character and lies in a context of a similar distinctive character. I think that it is this distinctive character of the empirical instance and of its setting which explains why our concepts are sensitizing and not definitive. In handling an empirical instance of a concept for purposes of study or analysis we do not, and apparently cannot meaningfully, confine our consideration of it strictly to what is covered by the abstract reference of the concept. We do not cleave aside what gives each instance its peculiar character and restrict ourselves to what it has in common with the other instances in the class covered by the concept. To the contrary, we seem forced to reach what is common by accepting and using what is distinctive to the given empirical instance. In other words, what is common (i.e., what the concept refers to) is expressed in a distinctive manner in each empirical instance and can be got at only by accepting and working through the distinctive expression. All of us recognize this when we commonly ask, for instance, what form does social structure take in a Chinese peasant community or in an American labor union, or how does assimilation take place in a Jewish rabbi from Poland or a peasant from Mexico. I believe that you will find that this is true in applying any of our concepts to our natural empirical world, whether it be social structure, assimilation, custom, institution, anomie, value, role, stratification or any of the other hundreds of our concepts. We recognize that what we are referring to by any given concept shapes up in a different way in each empirical instance. We have to accept, develop and use the distinctive expression in order to detect and study the common.

This apparent need of having to make one's study of what the concept refers to, by working with and through the distinctive or unique nature of the empirical instance, instead of casting this unique nature aside calls, seemingly by necessity, for a sensitizing concept. Since the immediate data of observation in the form of the distinctive expression in the separate instances of study are different, in approaching the empirical instances one cannot rely on bench marks or fixed, objective traits of expression. Instead, the concept must guide one in developing a picture of the distinctive expression, as in studying the assimilation of the Jewish rabbi. One moves out from the concept to the concrete distinctiveness of the instance instead of embracing the instance in the abstract framework of the concept. This is a matter of filling out a new situation or of picking one's way in an unknown terrain. The concept sensitizes one to this task, providing clues and suggestions. If our empirical world presents itself in the form of distinctive and unique happenings or situations and if we seek through the direct study of this world to establish classes of objects and relations between classes, we are, I think, forced to work with sensitizing concepts.

The point that I am considering may be put in another way, by stating that seemingly we have to *infer* that any given instance in our natural empirical world and its content are covered by one of our concepts. We have to make the inference from the concrete expression of the instance. Because of the varying nature of the concrete expression from instance to instance we have to rely, apparently, on general guides and not on fixed objective traits or

149

modes of expression. To invert the matter, since what we infer does not express itself in the same fixed way, we are not able to rely on fixed objective expressions to make the inference.

Given current fashions of thought, a conclusion that concepts of social theory are intrinsically sensitizing and not definitive will be summarily dismissed as sheer nonsense by most people in our field. Others who are led to pause and give consideration to such a conclusion may be appropriately disquieted by what it implies. Does it mean that our field is to remain forever in its present state of vagueness and to forego the possibilities of improving its concepts, its propositions, its theory and its knowledge? This is not implied. Sensitizing concepts can be tested, improved and refined. Their validity can be assayed through careful study of empirical instances which they are presumed to cover. Relevant features of such instances, which one finds not to be covered adequately by what the concept asserts and implies, become the means of revising the concept. To be true, this is more difficult with sensitizing concepts than with definitive concepts precisely because one must work with variable instead of fixed forms of expression. Such greater difficulty does not preclude progressive refinement of sensitizing concepts through careful and imaginative study of the stubborn world to which such concepts are addressed. The concepts of assimilation and social disorganization, for instance, have gained more fitting abstraction and keener discrimination through insightful and realistic studies, such as those of W. I. Thomas and Robert E. Park. Actually, all that I am saying here is that careful and probing study of occurrences in our natural social world provides the means of bringing sensitizing concepts more and more in line with what such study reveals. In short, there is nothing esoteric or basically unusual in correcting and refining sensitizing concepts in the light of stubborn empirical findings.

It should be pointed out, also, that sensitizing concepts, even though they are grounded on sense instead of on explicit objective traits, can be formulated and communicated. This is done little by formal definition and certainly not by setting bench marks. It is accomplished instead by exposition which yields a meaningful picture, abetted by apt illustrations which enable one to grasp the reference in terms of one's own experience. This is how we come to see meaning and sense in our concepts. Such exposition, it should be added, may be good or poor—and by the same token it may be improved.

Deficiency in sensitizing concepts, then, is not inevitable nor irremediable. Indeed, the admitted deficiency in our concepts, which certainly are used these days as sensitizing concepts, is to be ascribed to inadequacy of study of the empirical instances to which they refer, and to inadequacy of their exposition. Inadequate study and poor exposition usually go together. The great vice, and the enormously widespread vice, in the use of sensitizing concepts is to take them for granted—to rest content with whatever element of plausibility they possess. Under such circumstances, the concept takes the form of a vague stereotype and it becomes only a device for ordering or arranging empirical instances. As such it is not tested and assayed against the empirical instances and thus forfeits the only means of its improvement as an analytical tool. But this merely indicates inadequate, slovenly or lazy work and need not be. If varied empirical instances are chosen for study, and if that study is careful, probing and imaginative, with an ever alert eye on whether, or how far, the concept fits, full means are provided for the progressive refinement of sensitizing concepts.

Enough has been said to set the problem of what is wrong with social theory. I have ignored a host of minor deficiencies or touched them only lightly. I have sought to pin-point the basic source of deficiency. This consists in the difficulty of bringing social theory into a close and self-correcting relation with its empirical world so that its proposals about that world can be tested, refined and enriched by the data of that world. This difficulty, in turn, centers in the concepts of theory, since the concept is the pivot of reference, or the gateway, to that world. Ambiguity in concepts blocks or frustrates contact with the empirical world and keeps theory apart in a corresponding unrealistic realm. Such a condition of ambiguity seems in general to be true of concepts of social theory.

How to correct this condition is the most important problem of our discipline insofar as we seek to develop it into an empirical science. A great part, if not most, of what we do these days does not touch the problem. Reflective cogitation on existing theory, the formulation of new theory, the execution of research without conceptual guidance or of research in which concepts are accepted uncritically, the amassing of quantities of disparate findings, and the devising and use of new technical instruments—all these detour around the problem.

It seems clear that there are two fundamental lines of attack on the problem. The first seeks to develop precise and fixed procedures that will yield a stable and definitive empirical content. It relies on neat and standardized techniques, on experimental arrangements, on mathematical categories. Its immediate world of data is not the natural social world of our experience but specialized abstractions out of it or substitutes for it. The aim is to return to the natural social world with definitive concepts based on precisely specified procedures. While such procedures may be useful and valuable in many ways, their ability to establish genuine concepts related to the natural world is confronted by three serious difficulties which so far have not been met successfully.

The other line of attack accepts our concepts as being intrinsically sensitizing and not definitive. It is spared the logical difficulties confronting the first line of attack but at the expense of forfeiting the achievement of definitive concepts with specific, objective bench marks. It seeks to improve concepts by naturalistic research,* that is, by direct study of our natural social world wherein empirical instances are accepted in their concrete and distinctive form. It depends on faithful reportorial depiction of the instances and on analytical probing into their character. As such its procedure is markedly different from that employed in the effort to develop definitive concepts. Its success depends on patient, careful and imaginative life study, not on quick shortcuts or technical instruments. While its progress may be slow and tedious, it has the virtue of remaining in close and continuing relations with the natural social world.

The opposition which I have sketched between these two modes of attack sets, I believe, the problem of how the basic deficiency of social theory is to be addressed. It also poses, I suspect, the primary line of issue in our discipline with regard to becoming an empirical science of our natural social world.

* I have not sought in this paper to deal with the logic of naturalistic research.

9

Science Without Concepts[*]

The title of this paper is not the choice of the writer. It has been conferred by the Program Committee of this Institute. As a title it is anomalous, since it seems to involve a contradiction of terms. It is probably designed to shock blasé and weary students—perhaps to insure at least one element of stimulation to listeners of what will prove to be a dull paper.

To speak of science without concepts suggests all sorts of analogies—a carver without tools, a railroad without tracks, a mammal without bones, a love story without love. A science without concepts would be a fantastic creation. Neither my understanding of my task nor your lines of interest would lead me to undertake to give substance to such a fantasy. I accept the title as a well-known logical device of revealing the actual by considering the impossible.

Let one think of any reputable science, and he will likely think of concepts. In physics one recalls the atom and electron, mass and matter, velocity and inertia, space and time; in chemistry, valency, isomerism, colloids, combustion, decomposition, atomic nuclei; in biology, heredity, environment, genes, unit characters, variation,

* Address given before the Ninth Annual Institute of Social Research, University of Chicago, August 20–23, 1930.

Reprinted from The American Journal of Sociology by permission of The University of Chicago Press.

natural selection; in psychology, habit, reflex, feeling, integration, the unconscious, inhibition; in sociology, culture, the group, cultural lag, socialization, social disorganization. The most casual survey of the history of any of these sciences shows a persistent use of such concepts. One can scarcely regard such concepts as survivals of earlier philosophical preoccupations, for one finds them in use today in the most exact of sciences. He who should declare seriously that science as we know it has no concepts, or has no use for them, presumably attaches some esoteric meaning to the term which science does not recognize.

Yet alongside of this picture of the constant presence of concepts in historic and contemporary science one may place another showing recurrent skepticism, and criticism of their use. Tough-minded scientists apparently have ever suspected an affinity between concepts and metaphysics. Frequently in their reflective writings they voice their belief that conceptual concern is the doorway to sterile philosophizing. That famous utterance of Newton, "*hypotheses non fingo*" is a classic instance of this attitude. Science clings close to real sense experience; interest in concepts is a philosophical concern.

There seems to be ground for this attitude of suspicion toward concepts. The sterile preoccupation of the medieval logicians and theologians with the notions of levity, gravity, wetness, dryness, actuality, and potentiality is a case in point. There are others: the ancient Greeks, for example, who, on the point of observing their world experimentally, "lost nerve," as Gilbert Murray says, and relapsed into comfortable cogitation over the inherent forms of things; the numerous treatises of philosophers on the physical concepts of space and time which physicists have long since found it best to ignore; or the still more conspicuous instance of the plight of social scientists in their efforts to construct a science out of their heads by elaborating the character of such concepts as society, economic man, sovereignty, progress, natural right, association, etc. In general, it might be said, scientific workers become sterile when they turn themselves to conceptual preoccupation. Modern science seems to have made headway only after wrenching itself loose from philosophical preoccupation. Its heritage is too precious to be jeopardized by a return to conceptual enterprise.

To oppose these two pictures is to set our problem. One suggests the inevitability of concepts in science; the other portrays the deep

154

suspicion with which conceptual preoccupation is regarded. Either view may be defended in polemic; their opposition suggests the advisability of showing the rôle of the concepts in scientific procedure, so that one may come to understand its functions, and, if need be, to protest its improper use. I propose to do this.

In outlining the problem I am bound to confess that my interest is in the function of the concept; in what it does, or rather in what it enables scientists to do. I have slight interest in the controversies as to whether the concept is real or nominal, whether the universal is being or pure idea, whether abstraction is a process of disclosing reality or of distorting reality. I say this because the bulk of the literature on the concept concerns such issues. Anyone with the interests I have indicated will find this literature dull and of slight value. It is possible to consider the concept as an incident or an episode of the scientific act and not as a detached entity. In that case, it is not important to specify its epistemological properties, but rather to consider its scientific use.

I think it best to introduce this account of the concept with a brief psychological discussion. Let us begin with the simplest situation: simple perceiving and conceiving. The individual, in orientating himself in his environment, perceives. What he perceives arises from and.ties back into his activity. It may organize him for effort; it may release or strengthen some particular action; it may lead to the abandonment or redefinition of a particular project. Perception arises in the interplay of activity and environment and serves to guide the course of the activity. However, not only may the activity be facilitated by perception, but it may be balked, blocked, or frustrated. The conceptual process is a mode of behavior, characteristic of humans, which permits them to circumvent such obstacles. When, in a situation, perception is insufficient, one can conceive the situation in a certain way and act on the basis of the conception. In such a case, conceiving serves the same biological function as perceiving; it permits new orientation, a new organization for effort, a new release of action. Further, if conceiving originates in the breakdown or insufficiency of perceiving it, in turn, flows back into perceiving, that is, the conception one forms will shape or influence the perception one gets. Conception is not merely a stop-gap to perception, but a fashioner of perception.

These simple points in the relation of perceiving and conceiving are familiar to anyone acquainted with functional and pragmatic psychologies. I submit that they are sufficient to answer our problem as to the rôle of the concept in scientific procedure. I mention them again: conception arises as an aid to adjustment with the insufficiency of perception; it permits new orientation and new approach; it changes and guides perception.

These points seem to apply equally well to the percept and the concept. The affinity of concept to conception and of percept to perception is psychological as well as lexicographical. The concept, in one of its aspects, is a way of conceiving. Mass, motion, electricity, atom, culture, gene, heredity, integration, reflex, probability, assimilation, etc., are ways of construing certain contents of experience. We can illustrate this in a simple way with the concept of electricity. The observation of the attraction by rubbed amber of light particles, of the turning of the freely suspended lodestone toward the north, of the repelling of light bodies coming in contact with an electrified body, of the galvanic reflex in the frog, of the behavior of the Leyden jar and the voltaic pile—all these were experiences which in the reflective consciousness of certain individuals suggested the existence of something not directly perceived. In this case, this something became known as electricity.

Perhaps it might be better to say that, on the basis of given tangible perceptual experiences which were puzzling, certain individuals fashioned constructs which would give these experiences an understandable character. As far as I can see, scientific concepts come into existence in this way. They refer to something whose existence we presume, but whose character we do not fully understand. They originate as conceptions occasioned by a series of perceptual experiences of a puzzling character which need to be bridged by a wider perspective. I hasten to add that the concept does not merely suppose the existence of something which bridges perceptual experiences, but it implies that this thing has a nature or certain character.

I think that if you will keep in mind specific concepts you will easily understand these points which have been made. Mass, motion, electricity, atom, culture, gene, heredity, etc., arise through man's reflection. They are not items of direct perceptual experience; they have originated as conceptions from direct perceptual experiences which have been puzzling and problematic. They serve to introduce order or intelligibility into such experiences. As conceptions, they imply a content conceived; this content may be specified, discussed, studied, and reorganized—as such we may say it has a character.

From my remarks so far you will see that I regard the concept as a way of conceiving and of having a content which is conceived. Treatment of the concept from either of these two aspects will show something of its function. As a form of conceiving the concept liberates frustrated activity and enables new action. In any field of behavior beset by problems, as is noticeably the case in the field of science, this function is particularly significant. It requires probably little elaboration. On the bare psychological side, without concepts, activity would be tied to a given perceptual level with scarce opportunity of reaching a higher perceptual plane. Identical problems would be recurrent; there would be, essentially, no methods of gaining control over them. The world would remain constant; frustrations of activity would be suffered in recurrent fashion and would scarcely lead to any reorganization of the given content of experience. Such existence I suppose to be true in the case of animals. The worlds of man in general and that of science in particular are of a different kind. The reorganization of both in the face of problems can take place only by transcending, so to speak, the given perceptual world. In this transcendence the concept occupies a pivotal place.

For centuries the peasants of Europe and Asia suffered the loss of cattle through anthrax. This serious malady was a common occurrence. Many accepted it as something natural and inevitable. Others were puzzled by it and treated it as a problem. As a problem it was a recurrent one—the perception of the event was persistently puzzling and problematic. Scientists had studied the malady for decades, but their efforts to control it were balked. Release of activity waited on a satisfactory conceptual view—to be provided, in this instance, by Pasteur. It had been known for some time previous to Pasteur's interest in this disease that in the blood of the cattle stricken with anthrax were small rodlike organisms called "vibriones." These were regarded as interesting curiosities, but of no significance; they were epiphenomena of the malady. Pasteur approached this field of perception with a new concept—that of the infinitely small. This concept permitted him to organize experiments in a way previously unthought of, to show the specific influ-

157

ence of the vibriones, and eventually to yield solution to and control over the disease. This incident illustrates the way in which the concept as a way of conceiving may liberate balked activity. It also shows how in science beset with problems the concept releases and guides experimental activity and determines its direction.

Let me consider the significance of the other aspect of the concept which I have mentioned—the content conceived. As I see it, the concept permits one to catch and hold some content of experience and make common property of it. Through abstraction one can isolate and arrest a certain experience which would never have emerged in mere perception. Our perceptual world is one of particulars, for although conception is always involved, it is conception working through particulars. The abstraction of a relation from this world of particulars, and the holding on to it, is possible only through conceptualization and necessitates, ultimately, a concept. That is to say, the very act of abstraction is an act of conception; if the conception is to be held on to it must be given a name, a sign, or an identifying mark. By identifying such an isolated content, two developments of paramount importance for science are possible: (1) this content may become the object of separate investigation and reflection, (2) it may enter into the experience of others and so become common property. I propose to take up, in order, these two possibilities.

When I declare that the content conceived in a concept can be studied separately, what I mean is that one can take an abstraction which has been made, test and specify its characters, ascertain its range, and endeavor to determine more of its nature. I need not for the moment indicate how this is done in science; all that I wish to say here is that it is constantly being done in science. Through such study new problems and approaches emerge which make the concept all the more instrumental to a richer experience and a larger world. The point is a little abstract; let me illustrate it.

I choose, as a familiar illustration, the concept of motion as it emerges in the work of Galileo and Newton. As students of the history of philosophy know, in the eyes of the ancients and of the philosophers of the Middle Ages motion was not divorced from objects in motion. Motion was one of the inherent properties of the particular object. Thus, it was natural for a planet to move in a circle, for fire to move toward the sky, or for a heavy object to move toward a state of rest on the surface of the earth. Motion was definitely identified with particular objects. No one conceived of it as distinct from the happenings of these particular concrete objects. It remained for Galileo and his contemporaries in modern science to make the abstraction. In his famous experiments in measuring the swing of the lamp in the Cathedral of Pisa, in dropping pellets from the leaning tower of Pisa, and in rolling balls down smooth inclined planes, Galileo was making a definite shift from particular objects to general motion. The swing of the lamp, the fall of the pellets, and the roll of the balls were separate happenings; a distinctive kind of movement inhered in each. Through conception Galileo abstracted a content held to be common to all—a content which in being identified by a term became a concept. By conceptualization, then, the item of motion became detached and held. Those who are familiar with the history of modern science know that its development began in major part with the introduction of the concept of motion. Motion, as such, became a subject of experimental and reflective study resulting in the law of falling bodies, Kepler's laws of planetary motion, leading eventually to the law of gravitation.

I suppose that this one illustration is sufficient to reveal clearly the point that through the concept one may detach a content of experience and make it the object of separate study. It is only with this possibility that science may come into existence. Study instead of being diffuse may be concentrated; research effort may be focused on a circumscribed field, yet with the promise that the results obtained may be applied on a wide scale to many particular situations.

I return now to the other development made possible by the concept—the communication of experience. I have mentioned two significant aspects which a concept has: a way of conceiving and a content conceived.

The third aspect bulks large—the verbal character of the concept. The concept involves an identifying mark or symbol; so it presents itself as a word or expression. Energy, radiation, morale, competition, society, etc., are at least words. Some writers have said that they are nothing but words. As I see it, the word is an element of the concept, but not all of it. The word occasions a way of conceiving and stands for that which is conceived. The word, then, is a symbol of a given process of conception. By reason of its verbal or symbolic character, the concept may become an item of social discourse and so permit the conception that it embodies to become common property. A concept always arises as an individual experience, to bridge a gap or insufficiency in perception. In becoming social property it permits others to gain the same point of view and employ the same orientation. As such it enables collective action—a function of the concept which, curiously enough, has received little attention. It is by reason of the fact that the concept is an item of social discourse that concerted procedure is possible as far as science is concerned, and that a structure of science may emerge in place of a mere assemblage of disconnected actions.

Much of what I have said of the function of the concept applies equally well to common-sense concepts and to scientific concepts. To lump these together, as many would do, is to lose sight of the peculiar value of the latter. In showing the difference between them it will be possible, I think, to delineate more clearly the character of scientific concepts and show better their rôle in science.

To my mind, the chief difference is that the abstraction embodied in the common-sense concept is just accepted and is not made the subject of special analysis and study. Consequently, abstraction is soon arrested and not pushed to the length that is true in the case of scientific concepts. I should like to illustrate this with such a common-sense concept as burning. In ordinary perceptual experience people become aware that different objects will burn under certain general conditions. Leaves, twigs, wood, hair, grass, etc., when dry and coming in touch with some form of fire, will burn. This event of burning may be conceived as a separate happening; it may be designated by a word, and so become a concept. As such it has the advantage of the concept in guiding and controlling subsequent experience. However, it seems to be limited in the way which I have mentioned. Its abstraction is abbreviated. The smoldering of the manure pile, the spontaneous firing of the hayrick, slow combustion, the inability to get wet wood to burn, the smothering of the fire by casting earth over it, are incidents of common experience, but they either are not associated with burning or else are regarded as its limiting conditions. They do not raise questions as to what is burning, as a distinct happening, and so do not reach the point of modern scientific concern with oxidation and chemical transformation. The happening of burning is not singled out as an item for separate study and analysis. Of course, it is not to be expected that common sense would push abstraction to this point—there is no need of it. The common-sense concepts are sufficient for the crude demands of ordinary experience. Minor elements of inconsistency within experiences and a fringe of uncertainty can be ignored and are ignored. Hence experiences that might be productive of more refined abstractions do not arise as problems.

With such a background it is to be expected that "common sense," as the term strongly suggests, refers to what is sensed, instead of to what is acutely analyzed. This seems to be true in the case of common-sense concepts in much greater measure than in the case of scientific concepts; they are more a matter of feeling than of logical discernment. It seems that it is for this reason that an ordinary individual is puzzled when you ask him to define some common-sense term. He takes its meaning for granted; if pressed for its meaning, he is likely to resort to denotation, to pointing to objects of what he has in mind. Such particularistic indication is, of course, in no sense to be criticized. It does, however, show that the individual does not have the elements of his conception clearly in mind as separately comprehended items. This becomes apparent, if, in the quizzing of the individual, you compel him to stick to connotation. The meaning that he will give is likely to be very indefinite and vague, owing, as far as I can see, to the fact that he has not made separate study or scrutiny of the abstracted happening covered by the common-sense concept. It is not, perhaps, unfair to say that common-sense concepts are in the nature of stereotypes. Their meaning is just taken for granted, their character just naturally sensed. To question them is unthought of; indeed, to question them is to evoke emotion. So different is this from the tentative character of the scientific concept inside of the experimental field that it seems unnecessary to prosecute further the distinction.

What I do wish to emphasize is that the scientist is preoccupied with the relation covered by the scientific concept and because of this reflective concern opportunity is had for greater knowledge of this relation and so for the revision of the concept. When experiment is pushed into new domains along the line of the concept, one must expect to encounter new facts which, in turn, require a revision of conception and so of the content of the concept. Scientific concepts have a career, changing their meaning from time to time in accordance with the introduction of new experiences and replacing one content with another. Common-sense concepts are more static and more persistent with content unchanged. Since the abstraction covered by the common-sense concept is not made the object of separate study and of experimental testing, there is little occasion for the uncovering of new facts and so for the challenging and revision of the concept.

There is another difference between common-sense concepts and scientific concepts which strikes me as important. Common-sense concepts are detached and disparate; scientific concepts show "a strain toward consistency." The abstraction embodied in a common-sense concept tends, I think, to have an absolutistic, independent existence; the abstractions within scientific concepts are always being related to one another. It is no accident that concepts in a given science hang together in a system, nor that by so doing they make possible the structure of science. One needs only to think, for a moment, in the history of mechanics of the concepts of motion, mass, inertia, force, space, and time. These were interrelated and linked together in a conceptual pattern which made possible and guided experimentation and became the framework of the early knowledge and laws of physics. It is in the coherence of concepts, as I understand it, that one can get the meaning of the statement that science is systematic knowledge.

I have a suspicion that many of those who decry concern with concepts in science do not really wish to stop conception but are opposed to the building-up of a conceptual framework or structure. They urge us to cling closely to facts and confine ourselves to separate, specific problems. I know of no notion more out of harmony with the historic experience of science. To follow this program would mean not to have a science. At the best, one would have a series of discrete and separate studies, maintaining no organic connection with one another, fructifying one another only by accident, having but accidental strain toward consistency, and showing little that progressive accumulation of knowledge that comes with the organization and reorganization of experience. Some such picture is presented, perhaps, in the work of technicians, politicians, and statesmen, where concern is with immediate practical problems, where each problem must be given immediate solution, and so essentially separate treatment. Procedure is opportunistic, knowledge unsystematized, and control uncertain. But this is not the picture of science. Occasionally, to be sure, in the career of any science there may arise a crop of technicians coincident with the appearance of some new technique. With their technique as a tool they may move from one situation to another without conceiving these situations in terms of a larger framework and so without penetrating to or studying fundamental relations. They encounter generically the same problems, work in essentially the same fashion, and yield but detached bits of information. Such individuals may be called scientists because of academic affiliations; actually, they are mere artisans using the technique as a tool to the fulfilment of immediate ends. For mere purpose of illustration and without the desire to make invidious distinction, I suggest that such is the condition today of many statisticians. I do not wish in any sense to impute any inferiority in achievement to such individuals, but I would say that their work and results are unorganized and unsystematic. Unless marshaled and brought to bear on central conceptions or concepts, they would never attain the character of science as we are acquainted with it in historic experience.

The main points which I have made so far in this paper may be given here in a few sentences. The scientific concept, as a way of conceiving, enables one to circumvent problems of perceptual experience; the content of the scientific concept consists of an abstracted relation which becomes the subject of separate and intensive study; the concept, because of its verbal character, may be shared, and so it permits concerted activity in scientific procedure; scientific concepts in their interrelation make possible the structure of science.

I propose now to look at the matter from a new angle and to consider not so much what the concept permits but what it does in science.

As I see it, the concept more specifically considered serves three functions: (1) it introduces a new orientation or point of view; (2) it serves as a tool, or as a means of transacting business with one's environment; (3) it makes possible deductive reasoning and so the anticipation of new experience. Each of these three results merits separate treatment.

It is not a lexicographical accident that conceiving carries a double meaning: that of a way of looking at things and that of a way of bringing things into existence. That a new concept represents a new way of approaching the world is a commonplace. This is its intrinsic character. As an invention to fill a deficiency in perceptual experience it contributes a novel and original orientation. In the scientist's concern with his problem this new orientation and point of attack loom large. On one hand it permits him a flexibility in his attack on his problem; on the other hand, it sensitizes his perception and reveals the object in new aspect. Each of these two effects is implied by the other, but each may be considered separately. Those of you who have read any of the biographies of Pasteur will recall the new attack that he could make on his problems with the developing concept of the infinitely small. "Seek the microbe" was his proverb. The mysteries of fermentation, the silkworm disease, anthrax, septicemia, rabies, hydrophobia, and puerperal fever yielded to the approach made with the concept of the infinitely small. These had puzzled people for years, had been studied industriously, but had defied understanding and control. A new approach made possible by a new conception brought them to solution.

The rôle of the concept in sensitizing perception and so in changing the perceptual world may be neatly illustrated with the experience of Darwin while on a geological trip through Wales in company with the geologist Sedgwick. Bear in mind that this was before Agassiz had advanced his idea or concept of glaciation. Darwin tells us:

> We spent many hours in Cwm Idwal, examining all the rocks with supreme care, as Sedgwick was anxious to find fossils in them; but neither of us saw a trace of the wonderful glacial phenomena all around us; we did not notice the plainly scored rocks, the perched boulders, the lateral and terminal moraines. Yet the phenomena are so conspicuous that, as I declared in a paper published many years afterward in the *Philosophical Magazine,* a house burned down by fire did not tell its story more plainly than did this valley. If it had been filled by a glacier, the phenomena would have been less distinct than they are now.

This illustration is impressive in suggesting how conception may sensitize perception and yield one a new realm of objects.

Earlier in this paper I declared that conception arises from perception but flows back into it. The meaning of this remark is probably much clearer in the light of what I have just said. Through conception objects may be perceived in new relations, which is tantamount to saying that the perceptual world becomes reorganized. It is well to bear in mind that in the process new problems may arise, new techniques may appear, and new interpretations may suggest themselves. An entire new field may open up; scientific energy may be released in new productive ways. As I see it, this has been the experience of science on the adoption of a new orientation or, what is equivalent, on the adoption of a new conceptual framework. A conspicuous case which may be given in illustration is the origin of modern physics. The work of Galileo is usually chosen, with good reason, as marking the change from the metaphysical preoccupation of the medieval logicians to the scientific endeavors of modern scientists. His work is significant not only for the introduction of experimental technique but also for the development of new concepts which became the basis for the new attack of modern physics. These concepts are familiar. Mass, motion, inertia, force, impenetrability, etc., came to take the place of the concepts of the medieval logicians: essence, quality, substance, potentiality, etc. They provided a new perspective; they opened up a new field of endeavor. They raised new problems and suggested new techniques; they sensitized perception to new relations and guided it along new directions; they made experimentation possible, and ultimately they yielded new forms of control. A similar picture, I suppose, is being presented in contemporary physics in the new orientation and conceptual framework surrounding the work in relativity and quantum relations.

To construe our own discipline from this point of view is not without interest. I suspect that the milling and halting condition of our own science does not come directly from the inadequacy of our techniques, as almost everyone contends, but from the inadequacy of our point of view. The effort to rescue the discipline by increasing occupation with method and by the introduction of precision devices is, I venture to suggest, working along the wrong direction. Perhaps, like other sciences in the past, we await a conceptual framework which will orientate our activities into productive channels.

Let me turn to the second specified function of the concept. The expression, "Concept is a tool," is probably the one that we hear most. Its meaning should be clear in the light of what has been said concerning the aid which conception gives to the release and completion of activity. This function defines the character of the concept, for it means that it becomes instrumental to activity. The conception, in filling the deficiency in perception, not only provides new orientation and releases activity but directs such activity, either effectively or ineffectively. The success of the activity to which it gives rise becomes the test of the effectiveness of the concept. The concept is thus bounded on one side by frustrated activity and on the other by consequences which arise from the activity to which it gives direction. In so far as it lies between these portions of an act it has the characteristics of a tool. At first, like all tools, it may be crude and may be used quite experimentally; later, like perfected tools, it may become refined and its use quite standardized.

A few words about both of these stages—the initial trial stage and the highly refined stage—will permit one to see more clearly the instrumental character of the concept. In the first stage, the concept represents merely a primitive conception applied to some situation requiring solution or adjustment. It is in the nature of a hypothesis; its value is suggested but unknown. It promises some comprehension and control, and it is used on the basis of this promise. It may be unsuccessful in this promise, in which case some new conception will perforce be adopted. In either event it represents a mode of attack or a plan of approach to the situation. Its analogy to the trial use of a primitive lever or ram should be apparent. In being refined the concept functions none the less to aid activity, but its function changes character somewhat. Its field of operations becomes more definitely understood, its possibilities better gauged, and the consequences of its use more secure. By applying this concept to some new particular or, stated otherwise, by bringing some new experience or situation inside of the domain of the concept, one can deal with this particular or situation effectively, in known ways. The physician called in to diagnose an illness seeks for symptoms which will enable him to make as reliable a classification as possible. If diagnosed as a disease or as a particular kind of disease, as typhoid or malaria, by bringing the particular illness under the given concept or, stated otherwise, by applying to the particular illness a given concept, treatment may be made. One knows that certain happenings are likely to be followed by others; that is, if certain things are done, certain consequences will probably ensue. Thus the knowledge of the use of the concept as gained in prior experience serves instrumentally in the new situation.

With reference to the third function I may repeat that one significant value of the concept lies in its possibility of deductive consequence. The aid which the concept may give to the prosecution of immediate inquiry is perhaps easily appreciated; its character as a logical premise with deductive implications merits, perhaps, a little elucidation. What I mean by this remark is that by reasoning from the concept one may gain a new perspective and visualize problems and procedures which transcend the immediate problems which have given rise to the concept and in response to which it functions as a tool. The most outstanding illustration we have of this projective character of the concept is the number system. The historians of mathematics have made it clear that the early concepts of number arose out of practical experience and were tied to it. Certain developments, which we need not consider here, permitted the use of number concepts in other than a mere utilitarian way. Deductive consequences of number concepts were perceived, and the implications of their alignment and interrelation with one another have given rise to the huge complex structure of modern mathematics, seemingly endless in growth. This growth has proceeded not always in empirical but in logical fashion, and seemingly has raced far ahead of experience. Thus formulas for numerical functions have been worked out which may lie idle for decades before gaining practical use. But if the structure of mathematics may grow logically and not empirically, outdistancing actual experience, its interesting feature is that it ties back so successfully into actual experience. So clean-cut has been this application to experience and so productive of control that it has given rise recurrently to views that the cosmos was numerical. Without doubt, all science on its deductive side seeks to approximate the ideal character of mathematics. Although no science has enjoyed more than partial success in this effort, the attempt signifies an appreciation of the deductive value of concepts.

So far in this paper I have stated what seems to me to be the function of the concept in scientific procedure. My remarks, perhaps, extol its virtues; one should not be oblivious, however, to its sins. I feel that there is room for a brief statement of the improper use of the concept.

As I see it, most of the improper usage of the concept in science comes when the concept is set apart from the world of experience, when it is divorced from the perception from which it has arisen and into which it ordinarily ties. Detached from the experience which brought it into existence, it is almost certain to become indefinite and metaphysical. I have always admired a famous statement of Kant which really defines the character of the concept and indicates its limitations. Kant said brilliantly, "Perception without conception is blind; conception without perception is empty." Concepts without a perceptual base are indeed insecure. Unfortunately, in current thought we suffer a tradition descendant from ancient Greek philosophy and medieval scholasticism which favors the gaining of knowledge through elaboration of the concept. The concept is regarded as having intrinsic meaning, to be extracted by proper cogitation. It is unnecessary, perhaps, to call attention to the tenacity of this tradition in the social sciences. Each social science has many protagonists or devotees who strive to attain knowledge by "manufacturing it out of their heads." They start with an array of concepts which, while abstract, are abstruse, and then proceed to erect a system by drawing out meaning from these concepts. The result is a pompous and formal structure which, however, is as hollow as an empty shell. The fault in their systems lies in the fact that the original concepts were mere constructs, ungrounded or tested in empirical experience. Because of their original irrelevance to experience or activity it is not surprising that whatever meaning is drawn deductively from them is a mere gossamer, of no value for the understanding and control of the actual world. The difficulty seems to be due to a failure to recognize that the function of the concept is to bridge perplexed perception and to release and guide behavior inside of this perceptual field. To be valuable it must tie back into the activity, the break in which brought it into existence. It must be kept in relation to facts, its character tested by these and other facts, and its significance gauged in terms of its instrumental possibilities with reference to these facts. To treat the concept as an archetype instead of an implement, or to devise a concept which does not embody a plan of action with reference to certain facts, is to run counter to the procedure of modern science. Possibly such usage is not improper or unproductive in metaphysics; in science it is stultifying.

Not less abominable than this tendency to treat concepts apart from the demands and tests of specific kinds of facts is the tendency to manufacture them with reckless abandon, with no concern as to whether there is need for them. The charge has been made against sociology that it has the greatest number of concepts and the least knowledge. I hope never to be chosen to deny this charge and to prove the opposite. I suspect that this steady production of new concepts arises from the effort to pose as scientific and to be judged profound and learned. It is a common experience which I, at least, have in reading our literature to find the author taking what is already understood in simple language and translating it into more recondite terminology. This may satisfy a pretension to be scientific, but it in no sense constitutes a scientific procedure.

Another faulty use of the concept is to apply it as a label to an object of study and to believe that such labeling constitutes explanation and terminates the study. This vice—I call it such—is widely practiced in contemporary social science by both those who advocate concepts and those who inveigh against their use. Unless one comes to know something about the object that was not known before, there is no value in labeling it or putting it in a certain conceptual category. Much conceptual usage is mere labeling without yielding anything but the label. In the second place, to direct a series of conceptions toward an object, as one does when one applies a concept to it, is merely to orientate one's self for further action. To stop at this point is to miss again the instrumental character of the concept. One gets no control over the object, nor does one test out the concept as an instrument. On one hand, one does not know how much or how little the object is amenable to the use of the concept, nor how effective or ineffective is the concept as an aid to understanding or control. Such an approach is to remain on uncertain terms with one's environment and to block improvement in the instrumental character of the concept.

To treat a scientific concept in a loose, common-sense way strikes me as another sin. By this I mean to sense its content instead of to comprehend it; to be unable or unwilling to specify its character instead of being aware of its operational application. I had occasion before to distinguish between scientific and common-sense use of concepts; I might have added at that time that the latter form is not at all rare in science. Some workers in the field of science accept their concepts as ultimates, take their meaning for granted, and resent their questioning as foolish theorizing or personal attack. This attitude, by the way, seems to be more conspicuous of those who decry the use of concepts than of those guilty of over-indulgence. Because the former shun conceptual preoccupation they are unlikely to examine critically their own concepts, which, of course, they inevitably possess and use. Such naïve, uncritical acceptance leads to dogmatism and vitiates much thought and work. One might illustrate, perhaps, with the concepts of the subjective and objective. I know of few terms within the field of science used more lazily and emotionally than these. In almost every paper or discussion on method one will find them employed with abandon, and used, ultimately, as terms of reproach or approbation. It seems to me that these concepts in typical common-sense usage are taking on the form of stereotypes. I do not believe that their use in this fashion is of much aid to the logical discernment needed in scientific discourse.

What I would declare, then, is that to use concepts in science as natural ultimates instead of tentative convenient conceptions, or to be uncritical or unreflective as to their import, is not likely to lead to genuine understanding and control. Few things are more irritating than to read a piece of research conforming most stringently to accredited techniques and abounding in numbers, or units, or elements, only to discover outstanding sloppiness in conceptual usage. Others may be impressed by the proficiency in the use of technique, or by the clean-cut numerical relations between units, but I only regret our stereotyped methodological notions which permit and encourage students to play with mental toys in the belief that the manipulation of these empty terms constitute science.

Let us recognize the instrumental character of the concept inside of the field of science. By accepting it in this character and using it critically perhaps we can avoid being mere bookkeepers of facts or spinners of metaphysics.

10

The Problem of the Concept
in Social Psychology

The discussion in this paper is confined to concepts in social psychology, although the treatment will be of general relevance to concepts in the social sciences. The problem dealt with is the familiar one of the vague and imprecise nature of most concepts in social psychology. It is trite to point out that concepts which are vague and unclear are an immediate obstacle to effective scientific research and to the attainment of rigorous knowledge. For such concepts introduce a gap between theory and empirical observation and likewise do not allow for rigorous deduction. The vagueness of the concept means that one cannot indicate in any clear way the features of the thing to which the concept refers; hence, the testing of the concept by empirical observation as well as the revising of the concept as a result of such observation are both made difficult. Because of this difficulty in effective validation such concepts are conducive to speculation in the unfavorable sense of that term; the unsettled content of the concept encourages thinking to move along divergent directions without the benefits yielded by logical coherence. In these ways ill-defined and ambiguous concepts are damaging to both definitive theorizing and probative research.

It might be pointed out, further, that this condition of imprecise

Reprinted from **The American Journal of Sociology** *by permission of The University of Chicago Press.*

conceptualization lies at the heart of the scientific difficulties of such a discipline as social psychology. For, as suggested, it fosters a bifurcation of effort into the channels of detached theorizing and detached research. Such a separation—the antithesis of the productive interaction between the two in the natural sciences—throws open theorizing to the legitimate charge of being speculative and research to the likewise legitimate charge of being planless and frequently pointless.

Many students of the discipline of social psychology, repelled by the vagueness and confusion of contemporary interpretation of human conduct, have turned their attention away from theories and concepts. Attracted by the solid character of fact in the natural sciences, they have committed themselves to the search for exact data by the use of precise techniques, usually of a mensurative and sometimes of an experimental character. In taking this course they have been considerably fortified by an oversimple view of scientific procedure which would reduce the scientific act to a search for quantitative information and quantitative relations. The result has been a plethora of censuses, tests, scales, scoring devices, and minor experiments, all yielding a vast amount of scattered propositions. It is not an unfair judgment to declare that these efforts with their resulting information have done little to clarify concepts.

Many other students following the stream of an older tradition continue their efforts to explain human conduct through the use of common-sense concepts and the use of a variety of technical terms. Confronted with problems and kinds of human behavior which require some form of explanation, they apply common-sense ideas or any of a variety of psychological theories. Such efforts have the merit, at least, of choosing to grapple with what seem to be vital problems and of yielding some semblance of intelligibility to these problems. And such efforts, likewise, do gain some re-enforcement from the recognition that exact research, such as spoken of above, does not seem in its present character to be capable of grappling with such problems. Unfortunately, as a result perhaps of a faulty tradition and of possible intrinsic deficiency, the concepts employed in these interpretations are seldom subjected to rigorous test by empirical observation. The result is that concepts remain vague and the propositions which embody them become incapable of effective validation.

172

I take it that this separation between conceptual usage and empirical investigation establishes the major dilemma in our field. I take it further that this separation must be bridged if social psychology is to acquire the character of a scientific discipline or to yield knowledge that is scientific in character. To avoid all concepts which are vague and to confine one's self, as an alternative, to the quest for exact data and their relations is to turn away from the problems of the field. This pathway, either in terms of its direction or in terms of its accomplishments so far, does not promise a solution to the dilemma. On the other hand, to continue to form and to use explanations built around concepts that are not to be effectively tested by empiric fact is merely to perpetuate the problem. What is needed is a working relation between concepts and the facts of experience wherein the former can be checked by the latter, and the latter ordered anew by the former. Such a working relation, rigorously conducted, accounts for the development and progressive achievement of natural science; it seems to be essential to any discipline that aspires to the status of science.

It is this problem of the relation between concept and empirical observation in social psychology that I wish to discuss. We can start with the recognition that vagueness is characteristic of concepts in social psychology—vagueness in the sense that they do not have explicit features that would enable one to identify clearly the denotative thing to which the concept refers. To appreciate the point one has merely to think of such concepts as attitude, habit, temperament, personality, self, sentiment, impulse, drive, sublimation, extroversion, socialization, mental conflict, aggression, parent fixation, aversion, character, compensation, inhibition, social control, suggestion, and sympathy. Of course, one may point to some occasional action or condition of conduct as a clear, denotative instance of any one of these concepts. Difficulty, however, arises in an attempt to identify every instance that should come within the scope of the concept and in being able always to distinguish it from the instances that should not come within the scope of the concept. In other words, the concepts do not allow precise identification or differentiation.

One way, perennially proposed, of dealing with the problem of such abstract concepts is that of discarding prevailing concepts and securing a new set. This does not meet the difficulty, judging from efforts taken in this direction—for the same problem arises with reference to the new concepts. This, I think, can be appreciated by any comparison of different psychological systems. Further, some recognition must be made of the fact that many of the concepts, however vague, have arisen out of repetitive empirical experience and so point to some kind or aspect of conduct that cannot be ignored. Nothing is gained by changing the designation or label. The problem of the vague concept cannot be escaped by resorting to a new set of terms. The only legitimate occasion for the presentation of a new concept comes from the recognition of a new body of fact or from a new perspective which reveals such a new body of fact.

A second proposed way of solving the problem has been presented in recent years under the heading of the method of "operational definition." This method, apparently, would confine the meaning of a concept to quantitative and mensurative data secured with reference to it. Prevailing concepts—or at least some of them—would be accepted; counting and measuring devices would be used in the case of each concept; the resulting information would constitute the content and the meaning of the concept. Seemingly, such a method would yield a precise content, capable of exact test. However, critical consideration of this method should convince one that it does not offer a solution to the problem. It should be noted first of all that the method begins with the selection of a concept, which necessarily already has some meaning and some reference to an area of empirical experience. To limit this meaning to what is determinable quantitatively or mensuratively is essentially an act of reduction which may be at the expense of the empirical reference which the concept originally had and with which one is concerned. For it may well be, as seems to be attested by the results of "operational" procedure made so far,* that what is omitted is the most vital part of the original reference. The operational procedure, of the form spoken of here, could be successful in meeting the problem of vague concepts in social psychology only if the problems out of which the concepts arose and the items to which they refer were themselves essentially quantitative in nature. In present-day social psychology, only by an act of faith can one declare that the empirical problems and empiri-

---

* As a good example see Stuart C. Dodd, *A Controlled Experiment on Rural Hygiene in Syria* (Beirut, Syria: American Press, 1934).

cal items to which its concepts refer are essentially of such a quantitative nature. However vague may be the character of concepts in social psychology, unless it be shown that their nonquantitative aspects are spurious, the "operational" method is not a means of meeting the problem considered in this paper. As a means, of course, of helping to enlarge and to make more definite certain aspects of the concept, the method may be of value.

A word may be said here about a more extreme (as well as more logical) form of "operational" procedure that endeavors also to arrive at precise and unambiguous concepts. Unlike the kind of "operationalism" spoken of above, it does not accept existing concepts and merely try to make them definite by bringing their reference into quantitative or mensurative form. Instead, it would isolate some stable content (yielded as a result of some particular mensurative procedure) and regard the concept as any symbol that refers to this content. The symbol usually is an existing word like "intelligence," or a letter like x or y, or an algebraic sign. This procedure may be illustrated by the current view held by some students that "intelligence" is what intelligence tests measure. The argument is that intelligence tests do catch something that is stable, and in place of declaring that one does not know what is this stable content that is caught, one calls it "intelligence," and assigns it numerical value. Some points should be noted about this interesting means of escaping the problem. First, the stable content that is isolated has no nature; that is to say that the operation by means of which one arrives at that content does nothing more than indicate that there is something that is stable. The operation as such cannot analyze or characterize that "something"; confined to such operations, that "something" neither has a nature nor could it ever secure a nature. Thus, to illustrate, "intelligence" becomes merely a numerical value. Second, not having a nature, the conceptualized item cannot be studied—it gets its significance only through being related to other items. These other items (if one remains inside of the framework of this kind of operational procedure) would be other "somethings," also without a nature—presumably in the form of other numerical values. The relations between the items could be only in the form of quantified correlations.

What such a type of mathematical logic (into which the method resolves itself) could yield in the understanding of empirical life is unknown. If followed successfully, assuming that it could be followed successfully, it would result in an exceedingly odd framework of interrelated symbols. These symbols would be nothing like concepts as we are familiar with them, as in present-day social psychology. For the symbolized item would have neither a content capable of being studied nor a nature capable of generic extension; it would never stand for a problem to be investigated nor have any evolutionary development. To apply such symbols to human conduct as it is being studied by social psychology, one would have to work through concepts such as those we now have.* And once this step is taken one is thrown back to the initial problem of the concept. What this means is that the symbols arrived at by the procedure being discussed become intelligible and capable of application only through the use of another order of concepts and hence they do not displace this latter kind of concept.

A few brief remarks can be made about still another way of approaching the problem of the concept.† It seeks to arrive at precise definitions through a critical analysis of concepts. A given term is selected, its different definitions are compared, and its different usages are studied; the effort is to eliminate inconsistencies, to determine similarities, and, where needed, to classify or list companionate definitions. Through such critical consideration one endeavors to arrive at a precise definition (or definitions) which will make for common usage of the concept. This procedure is essentially a lexicographical effort and has value as such, but only as such. It does not meet the problem of the concept as that problem is represented by the need to secure conceptualizations that fit empirical experience. For it undertakes no study of the empirical field denoted, but instead considers the usages of terms; the empirical or denotative item enters only as it may happen to have been covered by the previous experience of the student making the critical analysis, or as it appears in the discussions of usages which are being scrutinized.

---

* This is done apparently by those who profess to adhere to the approach being discussed. Thus a person may view "intelligence" as what is indicated by intelligence tests and may use as its symbol some quantitative value, such as the intelligence quotient. In order to apply "intelligence," represented in this way, to human conduct, he has to think of it as standing for something generic, such as "problem-solving ability." In doing so he slips over into a different concept—in this instance a common-sense conception of intelligence.

† This approach is exemplified by the endeavors of the Committee on Conceptual Integration of the American Sociological Society.

176

The diversion of consideration away from the empirical item opens the procedure to the danger of becoming merely a formal elaboration of definitions such as we are familiar with in the case of "scholastic" theorizing. A scientific concept must remain in intimate relation with empirical fact and achieve its character through interaction.

The foregoing discussion has been given to show the inadequacy of proposed means of meeting the problem of the concept in social psychology. By abjuring concepts and so ignoring the problems for which they stand; by narrowly curtailing the area of empirical experience at the expense of perhaps more central forms of such experience; by tending to ignore the empirical factor and becoming a lexicographical undertaking—each in its own way suffers from some vital deficiency. It seems not unfair to state that each seeks to handle the problem by essentially avoiding it. For the problem is set in the need for an effective interrelation between thinking and empirical observation, and no solution can arise at the expense of either of these two factors or of their interrelation.

The problem to be solved has to be faced; and facing the problem requires investigation into the peculiar difficulties involved in applying concepts to human conduct. It is necessary to analyze the relation between conceptual view and empirical observations in this field in order to know what has to be done to improve that relation. The remainder of the discussion is given to this line of thinking.

The vagueness of a concept is equivalent to a difficulty in observing clearly the thing to which the concept is presumed to refer; indeed, this difficulty—knowing what to observe, being able to observe it, and knowing how to observe it—is the crucial obstacle in bringing the concept into touch with empirical experience. Consequently, it is necessary to consider the nature of observation as it is made of human conduct; for this observation involves peculiarities and difficulties which throw much light on the inadequacies of concepts in social psychology. The following discussion is devoted to the act of observation and will endeavor to point out some of these peculiarities and difficulties.

In the observation of human conduct one kind of item that the observer can detect and identify readily is what can be called the physical action—such as moving an arm, clenching the hand, running, cutting with a knife, and carrying some object. Such kinds of activities can be directly perceived and easily identified; designations or descriptive accounts of them can be readily verified. For, in the last analysis, even though they represent the application of a series of cultural designations, they can be translated into a space-time framework or brought inside of what George Mead has called the touch-sight field. Here people have common experience and therefore verifiable experience. Observations of this kind of behavior do enter into the literature of social science, as in the case of the anthropologist's account of technological activity. Being capable of effective validation, they do not become the cause of disputation. Indeed, they satisfy so nicely the need for verifiable data that one can readily sympathize with the behavioristic desire to limit observation to this sort. If all human conduct could be described by this kind of observation, and if our concepts denotatively referred to such descriptions, there would be little difficulty in having precise concepts in social psychology.

However, there is another kind of item disclosed in the observation of human behavior which is of a markedly different nature, as when we observe that a person is acting aggressively, or belligerently, or respectfully, or hatefully, or jealously, or kindly. This kind of activity cannot be reduced to a physical act or translated into a space-time framework and still retain the character suggested by the adverbs employed. It is such a kind of act which is genuinely social; and a great many of the observations that are made of human conduct are of such acts. The observation that detects such a kind of act is different from that which reveals the physical act, and, incidentally, is of a complicated nature. It is complicated in that it comes in the form of a judgment based on sensing the social relations of the situation in which the behavior occurs and on applying some social norm present in the experience of the observer; thus one observes an act as being respectful, for example, by sensing the social relation between the actor and others set by the situation, and by viewing the act from the standpoint of rights, obligations, and expectations involved in that situation. Or we may identify the act as being respectful by noticing gestures of behavior which are familiar to us in our own experience as signs of respectful behavior. Usually we observe the act in terms of both grasping the situation and by detecting familiar signs; ordinarily these occur together, although they need not do so.

It may be argued that the designation of an act as being respectful, hateful, aggressive, etc., is actually an inference and so is not properly a part of the observation. That it is an inference is, I think, unquestionable, but in many instances it is an inference that is fused immediately into the observation itself. This is true of every act of observation; even the observation or designation of a physical act is in the nature of a judgment or an inference. The only question is whether the inference will stand up in the face of a test. As I re-marked above, the observation of a physical act can be so validated, because it can be brought inside of a space-time framework. Simi-larly, the observation of a social act of the sort mentioned will hold up if observers have the same grasp of the situation in which the be-havior is taking place and, by virtue of a common experience, attach the same meaning to certain gestures in behavior. Where the situa-tion is immediately clear and where the gestures or signs are evident, the inference is fused into the immediate observation; if, however, the situation is not clear and unmistakable signs are not given, the act of judgment becomes less certain; in this case we tend to detach it from the act as observed and are likely to become aware of an inferential character or feature which we give to the observed act. So I am led to repeat that it is of no importance that a character that we observe in an act is lodged there through a process of inference—all that is of importance is whether the inference can be validated. Such a validation can be made in the case of the physical act, if need be, by applying to it a space-time framework which compels common experience on the part of observers. In the case of the so-cial act, such validation can be made only through a very different kind of common experience based on grasping the social relations in a situation and on recognizing signs of common human experience.

It is in this different framework, by means of which observation of social behavior is made, that we have the cause for the difficulty in getting agreement in much of our observation and the cause also of the difficulty of bringing our concepts to effective empirical test. A great deal of social behavior can be observed accurately in the sense that observers can readily grasp the social relations in which it fits or detect easily dependable signs present in the behavior. Under such circumstances agreement in observation may be reached. In the ob-servation of a great deal of human conduct, however, observers can-not arrive at dependable judgments or at a common judgment; the social situation which must be grasped may be highly complex and

179

pertinent elements in it may be very unclear, or the activity observed may contain no signs that permit an unambiguous identification of the act. I think that this can be appreciated if we consider some of the different kinds of observation that are made, or have to be made, in the field of social psychology.

As previous examples indicate, one kind of observation that is made of human conduct necessarily involves a judgment of evaluation. This is true particularly of social acts that take place in the field of interpersonal association; such acts may be observed in terms of the relations of the people toward one another or, as we say, in terms of their attitudes toward one another. We speak of a child talking discourteously or of a husband acting surlily or of a person treating an associate with disdain, etc. To cast out such observations on the ground that they involve evaluation is not only to ignore what is given to us in empirical experience but would do havoc to the field of social psychology.* Now, as stated above, frequently observers will form the same evaluative judgments and so agree in their observation. But, also frequently, as in the case of family discord, it is difficult to make dependable observations because of an inability to form evaluative judgments; our observations fall to a simpler level or else they become confused and ambiguous.

Another kind of observation in social psychology that becomes very difficult, but seemingly is inevitable, is that which requires the observer to form a judgment as to the intentional character of the act. One is led to infer such features as the meaning of the act, wishes, attitudes, tendencies, drives, impulses, thoughts, feelings, or character dispositions. This kind of observation is present in everyday empirical experience; all people make such observations; if they didn't, they couldn't get along. Theoretically, such kind of observation could be scrupulously abjured; but the question is, If so avoided, can one get descriptions of human behavior that are true to the character of empirical experience, that are of significance to such experience, and that offer any hope of handling the problems set by such experience?

---

* For one thing, practically the whole field of attitudes would be obliterated; for, as treated in contemporary social psychology, the attitude is regarded as some positive or negative inclination, which to be designated in any specific instance necessarily involves an evaluative judgment. It is a curious paradox that many of those who would argue vigorously for the elimination of evaluation in social psychology do a great deal of work with evaluative data.

To continue further, one should note that much of the observation of human conduct does not even get into the field of visual perception. Thus we may use as initial data of such conduct such items as a letter written by a person or the items which an individual has checked on a questionnaire, or we may observe that a person to whom we have sent a telegram has failed to reply to it. I think that anyone who reflects on the matter will realize that an enormous amount of the observations of human conduct are of acts that are not visually perceived but which we have to imagine. While agreement and verification may be reached for many observations of this sort, it is also true that many of them are uncertain, with a great possibility of error.

The few remarks given in these paragraphs to the topic of the observation of human conduct should be sufficient to suggest that the observations which are to constitute the initial data of social psychology are frequently very difficult to make, requiring complicated judgments and inferences which may not be dependable. Propositions based on data of such an inconclusive character become tenuous and difficult to validate. Or, to put the matter in terms of the concepts of social psychology, we may say that such concepts are vague and ambiguous because the observations that we use to serve them are tenuous and uncertain; and that the observations have this character because of an inability to form dependable judgments and inferences; and, further, that such undependable judgments and inferences are at present intrinsic to many of the kinds of observation which we have to make and use.

Set in this way, the problem of the abstract concept may seem discouraging; but, at least in knowing where the difficulty lies, we should be prevented from engaging in the practice of the ostrich or in expecting some form of magic to make the problem vanish. Obviously, whatever solution can be made must be along the road of securing reliable observation. But how are we to arrive at such reliable observation? We cannot, in my judgment, expect an answer by following any scheme which ignores the observational demands set by the character of social life. To confine our observation to the physical act would yield us dependable data, but we would have to ask, "data for what?"; seemingly, not for the problems which arise from, and are rooted in, a markedly different kind of observation, i.e., the observation of the social act. Further, to confine our observation to the simpler and easily detected kinds of social action could yield us dependable and verifiable accounts, but at the expense of the problems represented by the abstract concepts we have in social psychology. For such problems have arisen not out of the observation of such simple acts but of more complicated and more difficult kinds of observation. The answer to the problem, in my judgment, is to come not by changing the character of observation or by narrowly reducing the range of observation or by lowering its level but by improving the kind of observation that has to be made to handle the problems represented by our abstract concepts.

This last remark is something more than a mere platitude. For it means the need for an enriching of experience which will make it possible for observers to form more dependable judgment in those observations which give us our trouble. I don't think that there is any short-cut way of arriving at the formation of such judgments; it has to be done in the slow and tedious manner of developing a rich and intimate familiarity with the kind of conduct that is being studied and in employing whatever relevant imagination observers may fortunately possess. The improvement in judgment, in observation, and in concept will be in the future, as I suspect it has been in the past, a slow, maturing process. During the process the concept will continue to remain imprecise,* but it should remain less so as observation becomes grounded in fuller experience and in new perspectives. Even though imprecise, the concept will serve, as it does at present, to help direct the line of observation and to help guide the forming of judgments involved in that observation. That there is risk and danger that the concept may coerce the judgment and determine what is seen cannot be ignored; under such conditions there can be no effective interaction between concept and empirical observation. But we will have to run this risk—necessarily so great in the observation of human conduct—and seek to safeguard ourselves by viewing concepts as hypothetical and by widening our experience in the field to which they apply.

* In view of the nature of our problems, our observations, and our data in social psychology, I expect that for a long time generalizations and propositions will not be capable of the effective validation that is familiar to us in the instance of natural science. Instead they will have to be assessed in terms of their reasonableness, their plausibility, and their illumination.

11

Suggestions
for the Study of
Mass-Media Effects

A goodly number of social scientists and psychologists have studied the effects of mass media of communication. Their problems have ranged from narrow ones like comparing retention between oral and visual presentations to broad ones like determining the influence of mass media on voting behavior. Similarly their plans of inquiry range from broad exploration to exacting, if simulated, experiment. In spite of the variety of the studies, a basic similarity underlies the way in which the problem is approached. The student identifies the influence in the medium which he wishes to study, he identifies the people who are subject to this influence, and he seeks to ascertain the effects that result from the play of the given influence on the given universe of people.

Nothing would seem more natural or proper than to approach the problem for study in this manner. One pins down the influence, the people being influenced, and the results of the influence. This "pinning down" of the three objects of concern is customarily made by following the logic of "variable analysis." The aim is to make each of the three objects as precise and detached as possible. The medium-influence, as an independent variable, is isolated in a clean-cut fashion so that it stands forth as a discrete and qualitatively inde-

Reprinted by permission from Eugene Burdick and Arthur Brodbeck, American Voting Behavior *(New York: Free Press-Macmillan, 1959).*

183

pendent item. The people on whom the influence operates are given a fixed qualitative composition in such terms as age, sex, nationality, and socioeconomic status. The behavior presumed to result from the medium-influence is treated as a specific and qualitatively homogeneous item or series of items. The purpose of the study is to isolate a definitive and stable relation between these three objects, so that one may say that a specific medium-influence playing on a specific type of population will have such and such a specific result. To increase the likelihood of such a definitive finding, efforts are made to draw an accurate sample of the population, to eliminate or stabilize other influences that may be playing on the population, to use control groups, and to cast the independent and dependent variables into the form of quantitative units. It is believed that, if the study meets these methodological desiderata, the changes noted in the dependent variable represent the effect of the independent variable under the conditions specified. From such findings a set of generalizations is constructed on the influence of mass media.

This simple framework of inquiry, so characteristic of research into the effects of mass media, seems to be open to question. I wish to present reasons for suspecting that it does not faithfully reflect the operation of mass media in the real world, that it gives rise to the setting of fictitious problems, and that it favors false generalization.

The explanation of these suspicions must begin with a commonplace characterization of mass media and of the world of their operation. There are three simple features that need to be noted and discussed: (1) the variability in the presentations, or so-called "content" of the media; (2) the variability in the responsiveness of people due chiefly to an intervening process of definition; and (3) the interdependent connection of all forms of communication.

What is presented through mass media—the so-called "content"—varies enormously and continually. This variation becomes obvious not only by comparing the media but also by examining the content of any one of them. I am not referring merely to different kinds of material in a given medium as in a newspaper with front-page news, editorials, financial page, and sport section. Instead, the reference is more to the varying character of what is presented from day to day in any one of the component parts. This changing character of the presentations is true obviously of all mass media—motion pictures, newspapers, radio programs, and television programs. Mass media are geared to a moving world; all of them seek, so to speak, new presentations and indeed are forced to give such new presentations. The professionals who man the media and are responsible for what is presented are under pressure to offer something new and different; satisfying such a demand is part of their job. These commonplace observations show clearly that what is presented by mass media is highly diverse and undergoing continual alteration. What their "audiences" see, hear, and read is essentially always changing.

Next, a similar variation exists in the sensitivity or responsiveness of the people touched by mass media. By now students of mass communication realize that effects cannot be safely gauged from the "manifest" content of what is presented through a medium. It is necessary to consider how people in the audience are sensitized to the presentation and prepared to interpret it. Such sensitivity and responsiveness differ not only between people in the given audience but more importantly in given people through time. People are caught up in a world of moving events, which foster new objects of preoccupation, new lines of judgment, and new orientation of feeling. As issues arise or subside, as new interests emerge or recede, as sophistication replaces naïveté, or in many other ways, people shift in their sensitivity to presentations and in their interpretation of them.

Finally, the different media of communication are interdependent. They deal to a considerable extent with the same series of happenings; the producers in each medium are familiar with what is presented in the other media and are guided in measure by such presentations; further, people usually attend to a number of media and thus merge in experience different presentations of the same things. The consequence is that the media cannot be regarded as operating in separate and clearly demarcated areas, but rather as flowing into a vast common arena. For instance, much of what is handled in the press is treated over radio and through television, and is considered, further, in conversation and local speech. What emerges as striking in local discourse may gain expression or reflection in mass media. All major channels and forms of communication are intertwined in a vast communicative process.

The variation in presentations, the variation in responsiveness, and the interdependency of media challenge seriously the methodological scheme which, as explained above, is followed in practically all research into the effects of mass media. As suggested above, this prevailing scheme presupposes the following: (1) the isolation of an independent variable, consisting of the given form of communication under study; (2) the identification of the given universe of people and of the given type of their behavior subject to the play of the form of communication; and (3) the identification of the resulting influence, or so-called "dependent" variable. Under the scheme the independent variable is necessarily qualitatively homogeneous, constant, and disparate; also, the universe of people, their given type of behavior, and the surrounding conditions are treated as set and as having a logical constancy.

This scheme is brought into question by the shifting nature of presentation, sensitivity, and interconnection. It is highly doubtful if the type of communication chosen for study can be taken as qualitatively homogeneous, constant, and disparate; and it is doubtful if the people constituting the universe of study can be regarded as constant in their sensitivity and responsiveness. Let me spell this out further.

The varying and changing nature of what is presented by mass media does not favor the setting up of an independent variable with the true characteristics of homogeneity and constancy. Further, the intertwined and interacting nature of diverse forms of communication robs any of them of disparateness. Because of these conditions the setting of problems in the study of the effects of mass media has all too frequently a spurious character. Let me illustrate by referring to the current interest in studying the effects of mass media on voting. In such study some students seriously entertain the intention of treating mass media, collectively, as an independent variable, so that one could say that the effects exercised by mass media on voting behavior are such and such. This is as ridiculous as asking what the effects of conversation on voting behavior are. Like the content of conversation, the presentations made through mass media differ greatly in substance and manner and, further, are likely to evolve and change to meet newly developing conditions. Thus, to treat mass media as a single, homogeneous, and constant factor is to ignore their real character. Obviously, the same difficulty exists in selecting any single medium as an independent variable, as in recent studies designed to determine the effects of television on voting. Here again, the variable and changing character of the presentations whose influence one seeks to ascertain clearly robs the medium of the homogeneity and constancy that would warrant its treatment as a variable. This same difficulty holds for practically any influence that one selects for study. In every instance one is not handling the same presentation, the same condition of responsiveness, and the same setting.

These variations place under suspicion the frequent tendency to assert a given influence of mass media, on the basis of the findings of a study of some instance of their presumed play. This can be illustrated in a current view that the Erie County and Elmira studies by Lazarsfeld and Berelson show that the influence of mass media is restricted and minimal. Considering the wide range possible to media presentations, the wide range of the varying sensitivities of people, and the different possibilities in the moving developments in political settings, such a view is indeed pretentious. There is no established ground for taking the two studies as a representative sample of the universe of voting situations.

The form of setting problems here under criticism is further exemplified by efforts to compare the presumed effects on voting of different kinds of communication. The authors of one recent study, for example, venture a comparison between the presumed influence of mass media with the presumed influence of face-to-face discourse. Other students entertain an interest in contrasting the effects of radio with television, or television with newspapers. To set problems of these kinds seems to ignore what occurs in the real world. In a political campaign the various media are participating in a total evolving process, treating to a large extent the same events and responding to one another's presentations. What they present is filtered and organized in diverse ways in the experience of people, with much of it picked up and used in the arena of local communication. This intertwined, interacting, and transforming make-up of the communicative process stands in noticeable contrast to a scheme wherein each form or channel of communication is regarded as exercising a distinct influence that can be kept separate and measured in some parallelogram of forces.

Further difficulty arises because whatever influence is exerted by the presentations of mass media depends on the way in which people meet and handle such presentations. Their interests, their forms of receptiveness, indifference, or opposition, their sophistication or naïveté, and their established schemes of definition set the way in which they initially receive the presentations. Usually there is a further intervening stage before the residual effects of the presentations are set in experience and behavior. This additional stage is an interpretative process which through analysis and critical judgment reworks the presentations into different forms before assimilation into experience. This process of interpretation in the individual is markedly guided by the stimulations, cues, suggestions, and definitions he secures from other people, particularly those constituting his so-called "reference groups." Account must be taken of a collective process of definition which in different ways shapes the manner in which individuals composing the "audience" interpret and respond to the presentations given through the mass media. Although this collective process of definition may settle into a stable set of views, images, and positions, it is always subject to movement in new directions as people, collectively, face new situations, meet new problems and crises, and find it necessary to take account of new happenings.

Studies seeking to ascertain the effects of mass media are easily led to overlook the state of sensitivity of the "audience," and particularly the process of collective definition that is so powerful in shaping and sustaining this state of sensitivity. Generally, the student is inclined to take the audience as it is—to characterize it in terms of conventional categories of age, sex, religion, education, class position, and the like—and to assume that the responsiveness of the people in the audience is naturally tied to such categories. Even when the state of sensitivity is measured through a questionnaire or an attitude test, there is little realization that a process of collective definition forms the state of sensitivity and holds it in place. The failure to recognize and consider this process of collective definition leads easily to a deceptive generalization of the findings of one's study. A given group subject to an unusual and critical run of experience· may shift significantly its state of sensitivity without any change in the formal categories by which it is identified. A set of findings yielded by a study of the group in its earlier state of sensitivity could not be safely projected to the group after developing a different state of sensitivity. For example, it is readily conceivable, although admittedly unlikely, that the Elmira subjects in the Berelson study who steadfastly favored the Republican candidate could have been dislodged from this preference by some happening or series of happenings which brought disgrace to the candidate or to his party.   If the presentation of such happenings had occurred through media like the press, television, and the radio, an influence on voting behavior would have been attributed to such media quite different from that actually suggested by the Elmira study.   This is not a point of sheer conjecture.   There are indeed plenty of historical instances of profound shifts in the political preferences of people resulting from critical collective experience.   The possibility of such shifts, whether gradual or abrupt, should be respected by studies seeking generalized knowledge of the effects wielded by mass media.   This recognition is rarely made in current studies.   Indeed, it is largely precluded by the way in which the problem is put—one cannot allow open-ended variability in the setting in which the independent variable operates and hope to pin to this variable a set of specific effects.

Many readers will reject the foregoing discussion as having no merit.   They will argue that its criticisms could apply only to sloppy studies.   They will declare that studies rigorously designed on the model of the experiment and carried out with exacting care would not lead to the risky and faulty generalizations that have been hinted at.   Such an exacting and careful study would eschew the choice of a broad and heterogeneous variable such as a given mass medium and select, instead, something indubitably precise and constant like, let us say, the major campaign addresses of a presidential candidate. One would present these through a clearly defined and fixed medium like that of recordings.   The composition of the audience would be carefully determined in all relevant respects, including their "state of sensitivity" before hearing the recordings.   Use would be made of carefully matched control groups.   A clear identification would be made in advance of the precise area of behavior or make-up in which effects are to be observed.   The effects of responding to the recordings would then be carefully spotted in this area.   Any proposition resulting from the study would be cast in terms of precisely defined items—the presentation, the make-up of the population, the area of response, the given responses, and the degrees of difference between the responses and the original behavior.

Such a study would indeed avoid some of the sources of error and the faulty generalizations commented on in the previous discussion. But these virtues are achieved, unfortunately, only by sacrificing the possibility of generalizations that can be applied meaningfully to real-life situations. The exacting study establishes a situation necessarily unique, because of the rigorous restriction of the factors being dealt with and the resolute elimination of the conditions found in the real world. Whatever generalization it allows is restricted to the particular composition of factors embodied in the experiment. Because of the uniqueness of this composition, which is a necessary consequence of the design of the study, the results do not fit real-life situations.

Paradoxically, the more exacting the study and the more faithfully it adheres to the schematic framework of a precise relation between variables the less it allows generalizations that can be applied to the crude but real world. What appears as a paradox will be found, I suspect, to be a genuine dilemma. Students may be expected to continue their efforts to isolate an exact relation between a given form of mass-medium influence and its effects. In doing so they will strive to reduce their variables to items that are homogeneous, qualitatively constant, and clearly disparate from each other, for without these features the items are not true variables. They will endeavor, further, to stabilize the setting of the relation they are seeking to delineate, for without this stabilization they are checked in their efforts to establish a clean-cut relationship. Yet the very pursuit of study along these lines forces them to structure a setting whose parallel is not to be found in the real world. To generalize the results of the study to the real world is perilous, from a scholarly point of view, because the structured setting does not match a class of instances in the real world. Most contemporary students ignore or gloss over the question of difference between the structured setting of their study and the make-up of the real-life instances to which they project their findings and interpretations. More cautious students will face this question of difference and note that in the real world the designated items lack the character essential to variables and that such items are lodged in shifting and unstable settings.

The dilemma to which these remarks point is not inherent in studying and analyzing the world of mass communication. I suspect that it arises instead from the scheme used to make such study and analysis. This scheme, as suggested above, forces into being a study at odds with the character of the real world it proposes to study. Let me summarize some of the chief points of variation. First, the medium-influence has to be treated necessarily as a discreet and qualitatively constant item; whereas, in real life it is interwoven with other communicative factors and is subject to a flow of change in its content. Second, the audience or population exposed to the medium-influence has to be treated as having a fixed and constant composition; whereas, in the actual world it has a shifting composition. Third, and more important, the effect of the medium-influence on the "audience" has to be taken as direct and necessary under the specified conditions; whereas, in actual experience the medium-influence is subject to variable interpretation by the people before its effect is set. And, fourth, the scheme presupposes logically a world composed of set factors arranged in set relations; whereas, the real world of media communication is caught up in dynamic transformation of experience, of factors, and of relationship.

What seems to be needed is a different scheme of analysis—one that will respect the central features of the mass communicative process as it exists in the world of real happening. This process is not an addition or combination of single lines of influence coming from discrete and fixed items acting on a fixed and neutral audience and leading necessarily to specific changes. Instead, as mentioned earlier in this chapter, the features of this process seem to be: the variant and changing character of the presentations of the media, the variant and changing character of the sensitivities of people touched by the media, the process of interpretation that intervenes beween the presentation and its effect, the interdependent relationship between forms of communication, and the incorporation of media, presentations, and people in a world of moving events that imparts an evolving character to each of them. To study such a world implies the following: (1) the items used for study and analysis should not be treated as discrete but should be caught in their interlaced position—the aim should not be to isolate cleanly such an item but to handle it with its lines of attachment; (2) the items must be construed not as qualitatively constant but recognized as undergoing formation; (3) the "audience" or people must be viewed not as responding to stimuli but as forging definitions inside their experience; and (4) the network of relations must be seen and taken as involved in a developing process and thus moving out along new directions.

It is not easy to devise a convenient research model to accommodate these features. It calls for a perspective, a way of setting problems, a type of sampling, and a manner of selecting data that are alien to those found in current procedure. The construction of an appropriate model is a hope of the future. I wish merely to enumerate and comment on some of the principal considerations that should guide the task.

(1) A study of the effects of media-influence should seek to reflect accurately the empirical world in which the influence is operating. This interest should be paramount in place of an adherence to conventional procedure.

(2) An effort should be made to determine the state of sensitivity of people toward the media-influence. This means a need of catching the dispositions of such people in the form of their developing experiences. The roots of their sensitivity will extend back into a body of previous experience that has given some structure to their interests, their views, and their feelings. This previous experience has been involved in a process of interaction and interpretation between people as they develop orientations inside a moving world. In the flow of such previous collective experience, so-called "eddies and currents" operate to incline the people to certain kinds of responsiveness. To determine the sensitivity or responsiveness of the people in any meaningful way it is necessary to catch it in terms of the moving line of its development instead of in the present moment. It is also necessary to note the sensitivity of the people as a collectively formed complex and not as a congeries of separate and detached lines of individual experience. The introduction of this temporal dimension and this contextual dimension seems essential as a background to the study of the effects of media-influence. Life in a mass society is a moving complex. Any faithful study of it must respect this character.

(3) Any given media-influence should be studied in relation to other influences which may be operating in the area of concern. In the legitimate effort to isolate the given media-influence it would be erroneous to block out of consideration other operating influences. The real experience of people comprises a combination of

the influences at work; to understand any one of them in operation it is necessary to trace its play *inside of the combination.*

(4) It is necessary to consider how the media-influence *enters* the experience of people rather than to turn immediately to its presumed effects. What is presented in the media-influence becomes subject to interpretation by those on whom it plays. A process of interpretation which involves the play of the suggestions and definitions coming from many other sources, particularly from one's associates, intervenes as a crucial stage before the establishment of the effects. This process selects features of the presentation, shapes them into objects, determines the kind of significance with which they are endowed, and guides the way in which they come to be set in thought, feeling, and action. This process of interacting definition should be traced in the fuller context of the moving complex of developing life of the group.

(5) In line with the foregoing considerations the effects of a given media-influence should be sought in breadth. To single out only one line of effects, even though this be the avowed intention of the study, may weaken seriously an analysis of the findings. For example, in a study of the effects of television presentations on voting intentions it would be highly desirable to include inquiry into how people are influenced on related matters by the presentations. Thus, findings on how the presentations shape views of the political parties aside from the candidates, definitions of issues as against parties and candidates, beliefs about politicians and ideas of political life—such findings put the voting intentions in better perspective and yield an account more in line with the context of relevant group life.

The study of the effects of media-influences with proper regard to temporal and spatial contexts, the joint participation of such influences in the experience of people, the moving process of collective interpretation made of them, and the wider order of orientation that results from them sets new questions of sampling, selection of data, and lines of analysis. It is hoped that these questions will come to engage the serious attention of scholars in this field.

To accommodate these five features, it is clear, requires a different type of approach, a different way of setting problems, a different scheme of sampling, a different selection of data, and a different form of relating data. The approach calls for a historical dimension in order to trace the line along which people become prepared or sensitized to respond to media-influence. It calls for an extended spatial dimension in the need of catching the way in which people are defining to one another the content of the given media-influence under study. It calls for handling the media-influence not in isolation but in relation to other sources of communication which challenge, oppose, merge with, or reinforce its play. The scheme of sampling should represent the "population" as a developing organization and not as an array of differentiated individuals. The data would have to be selected to reproduce a moving process and not to isolate disparate and simple relations.

It is hoped that such radical changes in the scheme of study, needed to remain faithful to the empirical world, will come to engage the serious attention of scholars in this field.

12

Public Opinion and
Public Opinion Polling*

This paper presents some observations on public opinion and on public opinion polling as currently performed. It is hoped that these observations will provoke the discussion for which, I understand, this meeting has been arranged. The observations are not along the line of what seems to be the chief preoccupation of students of public opinion polling, to wit, the internal improvement of their technique. Instead, the observations are designed to invite attention to whether public opinion polling actually deals with public opinion.

The first observations which I wish to make are in the nature of a prelude. They come from a mere logical scrutiny of public opinion polling as an alleged form of scientific investigation. What I note is the inability of public opinion polling to isolate "public opinion" as an abstract or generic concept which could thereby become the focal point for the formation of a system of propositions. It would seem needless to point out that in an avowed scientific enterprise seeking to study a class of empirical items and to develop a series of generalizations about that class it is necessary to identify the class.

* Paper read before the annual meeting of the American Sociological Society held in New York City, December 28–30, 1947.

Herbert Blumer, "Public Opinion and Public Opinion Polling," Vol. XIII (1948), reprinted by permission of The American Sociological Review *and the* American Sociological Association.

Such identification enables discrimination between the instances which fall within the class and those which do not. In this manner, the generic character of the object of study becomes delineated. When the generic object of study is distinguishable, it becomes possible to focus study on that object and thus to learn progressively more about that object. In this way the ground is prepared for cumulative generalizations or propositions relative to the generic object of investigation.

As far as I can judge, the current study of public opinion by polling ignores the simple logical point which has just been made. This can be seen through three observations. First, there is no effort, seemingly, to try to identify or to isolate public opinion as an object; we are not given any criteria which characterize or distinguish public opinion and thus we are not able to say that a given empirical instance falls within the class of public opinion and some other empirical instance falls outside of the class of public opinion. Second, there is an absence, as far as I can determine, of using specific studies to test a general proposition about public opinion; this suggests that the students are not studying a generic object. This suggestion is supported by the third observation—a paucity, if not a complete absence, of generalizations about public opinion despite the voluminous amount of polling studies of public opinion. It must be concluded, in my judgment, that current public opinion polling has not succeeded in isolating public opinion as a generic object of study.

It may be argued that the isolation of a generic object, especially in the realm of human behavior, is a goal rather than an initial point of departure—and that consequently the present inability to identify public opinion as a generic object is not damning to current public opinion polling. This should be admitted. However, what impresses me is the apparent absence of effort or sincere interest on the part of students of public opinion polling to move in the direction of identifying the object which they are supposedly seeking to study, to record, and to measure. I believe it is fair to say that those trying to study public opinion by polling are so wedded to their technique and so preoccupied with the improvement of their technique that they shunt aside the vital question of whether their technique is suited to the study of what they are ostensibly seeking to study. Their work is largely merely making application of their technique.

They are not concerned with independent analysis of the nature of public opinion in order to judge whether the application of their technique fits that nature.

A few words are in order here on an approach that consciously excuses itself from any consideration of such a problem. I refer to the narrow operationalist position that public opinion consists of what public opinion polls poll. Here, curiously, the findings resulting from an operation, or use of an instrument, are regarded as constituting the object of study instead of being some contributory addition to knowledge of the object of study. The operation ceases to be a guided procedure on behalf of an object of inquiry; instead the operation determines intrinsically its own objective. I do not care to consider here the profound logical and psychological difficulties that attend the effort to develop systematic knowledge through a procedure which is not a form of directed inquiry. All that I wish to note is that the results of narrow operationalism, as above specified, merely leave untouched the question of what the results mean. Not having a conceptual point of reference the results are merely disparate findings. It is logically possible, of course, to use such findings to develop a conceptualization. I fail to see anything being done in this direction by those who subscribe to the narrow operationalist position in the use of public opinion polls. What is logically unpardonable on the part of those who take the narrow operationalist position is for them to hold either wittingly or unwittingly that their investigations are a study of public opinion as this term is conceived in our ordinary discourse. Having rejected as unnecessary the task of characterizing the object of inquiry for the purpose of seeing whether the inquiry is suited to the object of inquiry, it is gratuitous and unwarranted to presume that after all the inquiry is a study of the object which one refuses to characterize. Such a form of trying to eat one's cake and have it too needs no further comment.

The foregoing series of logical observations has been made merely to stress the absence of consideration of a generic object by those engaged in public opinion polling. Apparently, it is by virtue of this absence of consideration that they are obtuse to the functional nature of public opinion in our society and to questions of whether their technique is suited to this functional nature. In this paper I intend to judge the suitability of public opinion polling as a means of studying public opinion. This shall be done from the standpoint of what we know of public opinion in our society.

Admittedly, we do not know a great deal about public opinion. However, we know something. We know enough about public opinion from empirical observations to form a few reasonably reliable judgments about its nature and mode of functioning. In addition, we can make some reasonably secure inferences about the structure and functioning of our society and about collective behavior within our society. This combined body of knowledge derived partly from direct empirical observation and partly from reasonable inference can serve appropriately as means of judging and assessing current public opinion polling as a device for studying public opinion.

Indeed, the features that I wish to note about public opinion and its setting are so obvious and commonplace that I almost blush to call them to the attention of this audience. I would not do so were it not painfully clear that the students of current public opinion polling ignore them either wittingly or unwittingly in their whole research procedure. I shall indicate by number the features to be noted.

(1) Public opinion must obviously be recognized as having its setting in a society and as being a function of that society in operation. This means, patently, that public opinion gets its form from the social framework in which it moves and from the social processes in play in that framework; also that the function and role of public opinion is determined by the part it plays in the operation of the society. If public opinion is to be studied in any realistic sense its depiction must be faithful to its empirical character. I do not wish to be redundant but I find it necessary to say that the empirical character of public opinion is represented by its composition and manner of functioning as a part of a society in operation.

(2) As every sociologist ought to know and as every intelligent layman does know, a society has an organization. It is not a mere aggregation of disparate individuals. A human society is composed of diverse kinds of functional groups. In our American society illustrative instances of functional groups are a corporation, a trade association, a labor union, an ethnic group, a farmer's organization. To a major extent our total collective life is made up of the actions and acts of such groups. These groups are oriented in different direc-

tions because of special interests. These groups differ in terms of their strategic position in the society and in terms of opportunities to act. Accordingly, they differ in terms of prestige and power. As functional groups, that is to say as groups acting individually in some corporate or unitary sense, such groups necessarily have to have some organization—some leadership, some policy makers, some individuals who speak on behalf of the group, and some individuals who take the initiative in acting on behalf of the group.

(3) Such functional groups, when they act, have to act through the channels which are available in the society. If the fate of the proposed acts depends on the decisions of individuals or groups who are located at strategic points in the channels of action, then influence and pressure is brought to bear directly or indirectly on such individuals or groups who make the decisions. I take it that this realistic feature of the operation of our American society requires little explication. If an action embodying the interests of a functional group such as a farmers' organization depends for its realization on decisions of Congressmen or a bureau or a set of administrators, then efforts on behalf of that action will seek to influence such Congressmen, bureau, or administrators. Since in every society to some degree, and in our American society to a large degree, there are individuals, committees, boards, legislators, administrators, and executives who have to make the decisions affecting the outcome of the actions of functional groups, such key people become the object of direct and indirect influence or pressure.

(4) The key individuals referred to who have to make the crucial decisions are almost inevitably confronted with the necessity of *assessing* the various influences, claims, demands, urgings, and pressures that are brought to bear on them. Insofar as they are responsive and responsible they are bound to make such an assessment in the process of arriving at their decisions. Here I want to make the trite remark that in making their assessment these key individuals take into account what they judge to be worthy of being taken into account.

(5) The above points give a crude but essential realistic picture of certain important ways in which our society operates. The fifth feature I wish to note is that public opinion is formed and expressed in large measure through these ways of societal operation. This point requires a little elaboration. The formation of public opinion

occurs as a function of a society in operation. I state the matter in that way to stress that the formation of public opinion does not occur through an interaction of disparate individuals who share equally in the process. Instead the formation of public opinion reflects the functional composition and organization of society. The formation of public opinion occurs in large measure through the interaction of groups. I mean nothing esoteric by this last remark. I merely refer to the common occurrence of the leaders or officials of a functional group taking a stand on behalf of the group with reference to an issue and voicing explicitly or implicitly this stand on behalf of the group. Much of the interaction through which public opinion is formed is through the clash of these group views and positions. In no sense does such a group view imply that it is held in equal manner and in equal degree by all of the members of the group. Many of the members of the group may subscribe to the view without understanding it, many may be indifferent about it, many may share the view only in part, and many may actually not share the view but still not rebel against the representatives of the group who express the view. Nevertheless the view, as indicated, may be introduced into the forum of discussion as the view of the group and may be reacted to as such. To bring out this point in another way, one need merely note that in the more outstanding expressions of view on an issue, the individuals almost always speak either explicitly or implicitly as representatives of groups. I would repeat that in any realistic sense the diversified interaction which gives rise to public opinion is in large measure between functional groups and not merely between disparate individuals.

I think that it is also very clear that in the process of forming public opinion, individuals are not alike in influence nor are groups that are equal numerically in membership alike in influence. This is so evident as not to require elaboration. It is enough merely to point out that differences in prestige, position, and influence that characterize groups and individuals in the functional organizations of a society are brought into play in the formation of public opinion.

The picture of a series of groups and individuals of significantly different influence interacting in the formation of public opinion holds true equally well with reference to the expression of public opinion. By expression of public opinion I mean bringing the public opinion to bear on those who have to act in response to public opinion. This expression is not in the form of a parade or array of the views of disparate individuals, in an open forum. Where the views are voiced in open forum they are likely, as has been indicated, to be in one way or another the expression of group views. But in addition to the voicing of views in the open forum, the expression of public opinion is in the form of direct influence on those who are to act in response to public opinion. Through such means as letters, telegrams, petitions, resolutions, lobbies, delegations, and personal meetings interested groups and individuals bring their views and positions to bear on the key persons who have to make the decisions. I am not concerned with whether such forms of expressing public opinion should occur; I merely wish to emphasize that in any realistic consideration of public opinion it must be recognized that such means of expressing public opinion do occur. A society which has to act will use the channels of action that it has in its structure.

(6) The last feature of public opinion that I wish to note is that in *any realistic sense* public opinion consists of the pattern of the diverse views and positions on the issue *that come to the individuals who have to act in response to the public opinion.* Public opinion which was a mere display, or which was terminal in its very expression, or which never came to the attention of those who have to act on public opinion would be impotent and meaningless as far as affecting the action or operation of society is concerned. Insofar as public opinion is *effective* on societal action it becomes so only by entering into the purview of whoever, like legislators, executives, administrators, and policy makers, have to act on public opinion. To me this proposition is self-evident. If it be granted, the character of public opinion in terms of meaningful operation must be sought in the array of views and positions which enter into the consideration of those who have to take action on public opinion.

It is important to note that the individual who has to act on public opinion has to *assess* the public opinion as it comes to his attention, because of the very fact that this public opinion comes to him in the form of diverse views and usually opposed views. Insofar as he is responsive to public opinion he has to weigh the respective views. How this assessment is made is an obscure matter. But one generalization even though trite, can be made safely, to wit, that the individual takes into account different views only to the extent to which such views count. And views count pretty much on the basis of how the individual judges the "backing" of the views and the implication of the backing. It is in this sense, again, that the organization of the society with its differentiation of prestige and power enters into the character of public opinion. As was explained above, the key person who has to act on public opinion is usually subject to a variety of presentations, importunities, demands, criticisms, and suggestions that come to him through the various channels in the communicative structure of society. Unless one wishes to conjure in his imagination a very fanciful society he must admit that the servant of public opinion is forced to make an assessment of the expressions of public opinion that come to his attention and that in this assessment consideration is given to expressions only to the extent to which they are judged to "count."

The foregoing six features are, I believe, trite but faithful points about public opinion as it functions in our society. They may serve as a background for the examination of public opinion polling. I may state here that in this discussion I am not concerning myself with the problem of whether the individual opinions one gets through the polling interview are reasonably valid. My discussion, instead, is concerned with the question of the value of poll findings even if one makes the dubious assumption that the individual opinions that are secured are valid.

In my judgment the inherent deficiency of public opinion polling, certainly as currently done, is contained in its sampling procedure. Its current sampling procedure forces a treatment of society as if society were only an aggregation of disparate individuals. Public opinion, in turn, is regarded as being a quantitative distribution of individual opinions. This way of treating society and this way of viewing public opinion must be regarded as markedly unrealistic. The best way I can bring this out is by making continuous reference to the common sense empirical observations of public opinion that were noted previously. We do not know at all whether individuals in the sample represent that portion of structured society that is participating in the formation of public opinion on a given issue. That the sample will catch a number of them, or even a larger number of them, is very likely. But, as far as I am able to determine, there is no way in current public opinion polling to know much about this. Certainly the mere fact that the interviewee either gives or does not give an opinion does not tell you whether he is participating in the formation of public opinion as it is being built up functionally in the society. More important, assuming that the sample catches the individuals who are participating in the formation of the given public opinion, no information is given of their part in this process. One cannot identify from the sample or from the replies of those constituting the sample the social niche of the individual in that portion of the social structure in which the public opinion is being formed. Such information is not given in the conventional items of age, sex, occupation, economic status, educational attainment or class status. These are rarely the marks of significant functional position in the formation of public opinion on a given issue. We do not know from the conventional kind of sample or from the responses of the interviewee what influence, if any, he has in the formation or expression of public opinion. We do not know whether he has a following or whether he doesn't. We do not know whether or not he is speaking on behalf of a group or groups or whether he even belongs to functional groups interested in the issue. If he does, perchance, express the views of some such functional group, we don't know whether or not that group is busily at work in the channels of society to give vigorous expression to their point of view. We do not even know whether he, as an individual, is translating his opinion into what I have termed previously "effective public opinion."

In short, we know essentially nothing of the individual in the sample with reference to the significance of him or of his opinion in the public opinion that is being built up or which is expressing itself functionally in the operation of society. We do not know whether the individual has the position of an archbishop or an itinerant laborer; whether he belongs to a powerful group taking a vigorous stand on the issue or whether he is a detached recluse with no membership in a functional group; whether he is bringing his opinion to bear in some fashion at strategic points in the operation of society or whether it is isolated and socially impotent. We do not know what role, if any, any individual in the sample plays in the formation of the public opinion on which he is questioned, and we do not know what part, if any, his opinion as given has in the functional public opinion which exists with reference to the issue.

What has just been said with reference to the individual component of the public opinion poll applies collectively to the total findings. The collective findings have no assurance of depicting public opinion on a given issue because these findings ignore the framework and the functional operation of the public opinion. If this is not clear from what has already been said, I would like to point out the enormous difficulty that occurs when one seeks to assess the findings of a public opinion poll in terms of the organization of society with which an administrator, legislator, executive, or similarly placed person has to contend. As I have stated earlier such an individual who is presumably responsive to public opinion has to assess public opinion as it comes to his attention in terms of the functional organization of society to which he is responsive. He has to view that society in terms of groups of divergent influence; in terms of organizations with different degrees of power; in terms of individuals with followings; in terms of indifferent people—all, in other words, in terms of what and who counts in his part of the social world. This type of assessment which is called for in the instance of an organized society in operation is well-nigh impossible to make in the case of the findings of public opinion polls. We are unable to answer such questions as the following: how much power and influence is possessed by those who have the favorable opinion or the unfavorable opinion; who are these people who have the opinion; whom do they represent; how well organized are they; what groups do they belong to that are stirring around on the scene and that are likely to continue to do so; are those people who have the given opinion very much concerned about their opinion; are they going to get busy and do something about it; are they going to get vociferous, militant, and troublesome; are they in the position to influence powerful groups and individuals *who are known;* does the opinion represent a studied policy of significant organizations which will persist and who are likely to remember; is the opinion an ephemeral or momentary view which people will quickly forget? These sample questions show how markedly difficult it is to assess the results of public opinion polling from the standpoint of the things that have to be taken into account in working in an organized society. This difficulty, in turn, signifies that current public opinion polling gives an inaccurate and unrealistic picture of public opinion because of the failure to catch opinions as they are organized and as they operate in a functioning society.

What I have said will appear to many as distinctly invalid on the ground that public opinion polling has *demonstrated* that it can and does detect public opinion faithfully, by virtue of its marked success in predicting election returns. This contention needs to be investigated carefully, particularly since in most circles polling, wherever applied, is regarded as intrinsically valid because of its rather spectacular success in predicting elections. What I think needs to be noted is that the casting of ballots is distinctly an action of separate individuals wherein a ballot cast by one individual has exactly the same weight as a ballot cast by another individual. In this proper sense, and in the sense of real action, voters constitute a population of disparate individuals, each of whom has equal weight to the others. Consequently, the sampling procedure which is based on a population of disparate individuals is eminently suited to securing a picture of what the voting is likely to be. However, to regard the successful use of polling in this area as proof of its automatic validity when applied to an area where people do not act as equally weighted disparate individuals begs the very question under consideration. I would repeat that the formation and expression of public opinion giving rise to effective public opinion is not an action of a population of disparate individuals having equal weight but is a function of a structured society, differentiated into a network of different kinds of groups and individuals having differential weight and influence and occupying different strategic positions. Accordingly, to my mind, the success attending polling in the prediction of elections gives no validity to the method as a means of studying, recording or measuring public opinion as it forms and functions in our society.

There is a very important contention in this connection which has to be considered. The contention can be stated as follows:

An election by public ballot is in itself an expression of public opinion —and, furthermore, it is an effective and decisive expression of public opinion. It is, in fact, the ultimate expression of public opinion and thus it represents the proper norm of the expression of public opinion. In the election by ballot each voter, in accordance with the basic principles of democracy, has his say as a citizen and has equal worth to every other citizen in casting his ballot. If election by ballot be recognized as the genuine referendum in which true public opinion comes to expression, then the preeminence of current public opinion polling as the device for recording and measuring public opinion is established. For, public opinion polling with its current form of sampling has demonstrated that it can predict reliably and effectively the results of the election. Accordingly, public opinion polling, in itself, can be used as a type of referendum to record and measure the true opinion of the public on issues in the instances of which the public does not go to the election polls. Thus, public opinion polling yields a more reliable and accurate picture of public opinion than is represented by the confused, indefinite, slanted, and favor-ridden expressions of opinion that come ordinarily to the legislator, administrator, or executive who has to act on public opinion. The public opinion poll tells us where people stand. It gives us the *vox populi*.

My remarks with reference to this contention will be brief. It should be evident on analysis that the contention is actually a normative plea and not a defense of polling as a method of study of public opinion as such public opinion functions in our society. The contention proposes that public opinion be construed in a particular way, to wit, that public opinion *ought to be* an aggregation of the opinions of a cross section of the population rather than what it is in the actual functioning of society. To my mind it is highly questionable whether in the day by day operation of our society public opinion ought to be of the nature posited by the public opinion poll. Many appropriate questions could be raised about how and to what extent public opinion is expressed at the election polls, and, more important, whether it would be possible or even advisable for public opinion, in the form of an aggregation of equally weighted individual opinions, to function meaningfully in a society with a diversified organization. However, such questions need not be raised here. It is sufficient to note that if one seeks to justify polling as a method of studying public opinion on the ground that the composition of public opinion *ought to be* different than what it is, he is not establishing the validity of the method for the study of the empirical world as it is. Instead, he is hanging on the coat-tails of a dubious proposal for social reform.*

---

* I refer to such a program as dubious because I believe the much needed improvement of public opinion in our society should be in the process by which public opinion organically functions, i.e., by arousing, organizing, and effectively directing the opinion of people who appreciate that they have an interest in a given issue. A reliance, instead, on a mere "referendum" by an undifferentiated mass, having great segments of indifference and non-participation, is unlikely to offer a desirable public opinion. At the best, in my judgment, such a "referendum" could operate as a corrective supplement and not as a substitute. The important question concerning the directions in which public opinion might secure its much needed improvement is, of course, outside of the scope of this paper.

In this paper I have presented criticisms of "public opinion polling" as a method for the recording and measurement of public opinion. These criticisms have centered around the distortion that stems from the use of a sample in the form of an aggregation of disparate individuals having equal weight. These criticisms should not be misinterpreted to mean that such a sampling procedure is invalid wherever applied or that wherever polling makes use of such a sampling procedure such polling is intrinsically invalid. Clearly, the criticism applies when such a sampling procedure is used to study a matter whose composition is an organization of interacting parts instead of being merely an aggregation of individuals. Where the matter which one is studying is an aggregation of individual units then the application of the sampling procedure spoken of is clearly in order. I make this banal statement only to call attention to the fact that there are obviously many matters about human beings and their conduct that have just this character of being an aggregation of individuals or a congeries of individual actions. Many demographic matters are of this nature. Also, many actions of human beings in a society are of this nature—such as casting ballots, purchasing tooth paste, going to motion picture shows, and reading newspapers. Such actions, which I like to think of as mass actions of individuals in contrast to organized actions of groups, lend themselves readily to the type of sampling that we have in current public opinion polling. In fact, it is the existence of such mass actions of individuals which explains, in my judgment, the successful use in consumer research of sampling such as is employed in public opinion polling. What I find questionable, and what this paper criticizes, is the use of such sampling with its implicit imagery and logic in the study of a matter which, like the process of public opinion, functions as a moving organization of interconnected parts.

The last item I wish to consider briefly refers to the interesting and seemingly baffling question of how one should or can sample an object matter which is a complicated system of interacting parts having differential influence in the total operation. Perhaps the question in itself is absurd. At various times I have asked different experts in sampling how one would sample an organic structure. With a single exception these individuals looked at me askance as if the question were idiotic. But the problem, I think, remains even though I find it difficult to state. In human society, particularly in modern society, we are confronted with intricate complexes of moving relations which are roughly recognizable as systems, even though loose systems. Such a loose system is too complicated, too encumbered in detail and too fast moving to be described in any one of its given "cycles" of operation adequately and faithfully. Yet unless we merely want to speculate about it we have to dip into it in some manner in order to understand what is happening in the given cycle of operation in which we are interested. Thus, using the public opinion process in our society as an illustration we are able to make a rough characterization as to how it functions in the case, let us say, of a national issue. However, if we want to know how it functions in the case of a *given* national issue, we are at a loss to make an adequate description because of the complexity and quick movement of the cycle of its operation. So, to know what is going on, particularly to know what is likely to go on in the latter stages, we have to dip in here and there. The problems of where to dip in, how to dip in, and how far to dip in are what I have in mind in speaking of sampling an organic structure.

I suppose, as one of my friends has pointed out, that the answer to the problem requires the formulation of a model. We have no such model in the instance of public opinion as it operates in our society. My own hunch is that such a model should be constructed, if it can be at all, by working backwards instead of by working forward. That is, we ought to begin with those who have to act on public opinion and move backwards along the lines of the various expressions of public opinion that come to their attention, tracing these expressions backward through their own various channels and in doing so, noting the chief channels, the key points of importance, and the way in which any given expression has come to develop and pick up an organized backing out of what initially must have been a relatively amorphous condition. Perhaps, such a model, if it could be worked out, would allow the development of a realistic method of sampling in place of what seems to me to be the highly artificial method of sampling used in current public opinion polling.